WOMEN'S GIFTS, WOMEN'S ROLES

WOMEN'S GIFTS, WOMEN'S ROLES

A Roadmap for Navigating the Debate over Women in Ministry

ANNA CATHERINE PISTOR

Columbus, Ohio

Women's Gifts, Women's Roles: A Roadmap for Navigating the Debate over Women in Ministry

Published by Gatekeeper Press
2167 Stringtown Rd, Suite 109
Columbus, OH 43123-2989
www.GatekeeperPress.com

Copyright © 2018 by Anna Catherine Pistor

All rights reserved. Neither this book, nor any parts within it may be sold or reproduced in any form or by any electronic or mechanical means, including information storage and retrieval systems without permission in writing from the author. The only exception is by a reviewer, who may quote short excerpts in a review.

All Scripture quotations, unless otherwise indicated, are taken from the Holy Bible, New International Version®, NIV®. Copyright ©1973, 1978, 1984, 2011 by Biblica, Inc.™ Used by permission of Zondervan. All rights reserved worldwide. www.zondervan.com The "NIV" and "New International Version" are trademarks registered in the United States Patent and Trademark Office by Biblica, Inc.™

Scripture quotations marked (ESV) are from the ESV® Bible (The Holy Bible, English Standard Version®), copyright © 2001 by Crossway, a publishing ministry of Good News Publishers. Used by permission. All rights reserved.

Library of Congress number: 2018948996

ISBN (paperback): 9781642372410
eISBN: 9781642372649

Printed in the United States of America

Contents

Introduction 1
Chapter 1: Two Ends of a Spectrum: Complementarians
and Egalitarians 5
Chapter 2: Grammar, Culture, and Bias: Unavoidable
Factors that Shape the Gender Debate 15
Chapter 3: Are Women Inferior? Sexism in History,
Theology, and Practice 25
Chapter 4: Rising Tensions: A Secondary Doctrine
No Longer 39
Chapter 5: The Disputed Pauline Passages: Interpretation
and the Search for Transcultural Principles 47
Chapter 6: A Woman's Role in the Church: Problems and
Inconsistencies 89
Chapter 7: Calling or Gifting? Biblical Definitions and
Distinctions 101
Chapter 8: Developing Women's Gifts: A Biblical and
Moral Imperative 109
Chapter 9: A Hidden Life:
Principles for Faithful and Fruitful Action 141
Notes 153
Acknowledgements 191
Further Reading 193

Introduction

FEAR NOT, YOU have not just picked up a book that seeks to have its readers—all two of you—burn their undergarments, give up shaving their legs, or boycott cooking meals. Rather, my simple hope in writing this book is to share with you the key lessons that I've learned from navigating some of the more challenging and unexpected circumstances in my adult life, particularly as a Christian woman endeavoring to serve in the church.

I began following Jesus at the age of eighteen, during my freshman year of college, and fifteen years later—now with a husband, a career, and two young boys—I'm no longer the same person. However, unbeknownst to me, during these same years and even before, the family of God (i.e., the church) that I had joined was changing here in America. A theological debate has been quietly raging for decades now, and while the effects of such debates are usually unfelt outside the walls of seminaries, this debate has real and profound implications for Christian women in their homes and in their churches.

To see what I mean, think back to the last time when you had to find a new local church or other community of believers. Both experience and Scripture have taught me that Christianity is not a solitary journey, and I would strongly affirm that all of us who are passionately pursuing Jesus Christ need to be engaged with a local community of believers to help us live radical lives for the sake of the gospel (Heb. 10:24–25). As you become involved in this community, getting to know its members and its culture, its values and its vision, something natural should start to build in your heart: commitment. As the bonds of friendship and fellowship grow, so does the desire to serve alongside spiritual brothers and sisters (Matt. 12:50; Mark 3:35). But if you're a woman, something deeper happens at a psychological level. Whether you realize it or not, you also internalize, often unconsciously, where women are permitted to serve and where they are not, when they are encouraged and invited to participate and when the task is left to men alone.

Do women teach Sunday school to adults of both genders, or only to children? Do women lead worship, or do they only perform as accompanying musicians or vocalists to a male worship leader? Are the elders, deacons, and pastors all male, or are there women elders, deaconesses,[1] and pastors? Do single women ever lead co-ed Bible studies, or are the studies only led by men or married couples acting together? If you're a woman, you probably know the answers to all of these questions just from simple observation, even if you've never stopped to consider them until now. These are real questions—real lines of demarcation—that every local church and parachurch ministry[2] must draw as a matter of practical necessity. But in the past few decades, the questions have taken on a new sense of urgency and seriousness, reaching almost a fever pitch.

So why me? Why should I tackle this debate over women in ministry, and why should you listen?

As you've probably already noticed from the omission of any credentials next to my name, I'm an amateur through and through. If you haven't just tossed this book out the window after reading that, let me give you a brief *apologia* (or defense) for the value of an amateur.³ An amateur can study many different arenas of knowledge, and occasionally⁴ this can lead to some new insight that only an "outsider" might discern.⁵ There can still be value from the contributions of those who study several disciplines to a lesser degree.⁶ The amateur can sometimes see from afar a small but overlooked detail that might help to better frame the discussion, even slightly. Indeed, that is all I propose here: no grand claims of cracking the code, the verse, or the context, but rather a thread that may be helpful to some or even one individual who struggles with this topic in a similar way. Please accept this amateur's humble attempt to wade through the scholarship devoted to this complex puzzle, and my attempt to forge a way forward for the benefit of others on a similar quest for answers.

So what *specifically* do I hope to add to this ongoing debate? First, I hope to add a fresh perspective on the debate itself, and also on the *manner* in which the debate is being conducted. I cannot firmly settle the role of women in the church and the use of their gifts in that setting, but the debate over the meaning of a handful of contested biblical terms and passages is one that warrants our engagement. In addition, I will demonstrate, using common sense and without resorting to the sometimes obscure methods of academics, why certain theologians have failed to meet the burden of proof for some of their more outlandish, emotionally charged, and aggressive claims.

We will begin in chapter 1 with a look at the two main theological camps on the subject of women in ministry, broadly labeled as "complementarian" and "egalitarian." In chapter 2, we will look at some of the major factors that shape biblical interpretation and affect the conclusions of the two camps. In chapter 3, we trace the issue of sexism back through the centuries, culminating in its recent elevation to central prominence within the past few decades. Chapter 4 will highlight how doctrines regarding women in ministry have moved up in importance to become "core values" at some local churches, and the resulting pitfalls of that move. In chapter 5, we will put on our elbow-padded professor jackets and evaluate the most pertinent scholarship addressing the key passages of Scripture at the heart of the theological disagreement between complementarians and egalitarians. In chapters 6 and 7, we will carefully consider two concepts, specifically "gender roles" and "calling," that are currently used by some participants to guide the debate, as well as the drawbacks associated with each approach. In chapter 8, we will look at the clear and unmistakable texts that call us to develop and use our spiritual gifts, no matter what our gender is. And we will conclude in chapter 9 with some guiding principles for developing our gifts and living out our convictions in a charitable and gracious manner.

After wading through the merits and shortcomings of both sides in the debate, it's natural to come away feeling somewhat uncertain, just as I did. This takes me to another purpose of this book. Specifically, the further aim of this simple study is to encourage women to recognize, develop, and use their gifts in a sensitive, charitable way to benefit the life of the church. While the debate may never be settled, there *is* a clear way forward—regardless of your interpretation of key Scripture passages—that involves using your gifts for the glory of God. And for that reason, there is always hope.

CHAPTER 1

Two Ends of a Spectrum: Complementarians and Egalitarians

And the problem in the church today is that it's just a bunch of nice, soft, tender, chickified church boys. Sixty percent of Christians are chicks, and the forty percent that are dudes are still sort of chicks.... The whole architecture and the whole aesthetic [of church] is real feminine, the preacher is kind of feminine, and the music is kind of emotional and feminine.... All the innovative dudes are home watching football, or they're out making money or climbing a mountain, or shooting a gun or working on their truck.... If you want to be innovative, how do you get young *men*?

—Mark Driscoll (2006)

There is neither Jew nor Greek, slave nor free, male nor female, for you are all one in Christ Jesus.

—Galatians 3:28

SOON AFTER JOINING a new church in our mid-twenties, my husband and I had the privilege of serving as leaders in the church's summer internship program for college students. For the students, this involved a mix of volunteerism as well as spiritual formation, Bible studies, mentoring, and the like. The weekly instruction was arranged topically so that the students were given the opportunity to discuss important issues ranging from the Bible to sex to money. However, even all these years later, one topic still vividly stands out to me: "Biblical Manhood and Womanhood."

Sunny, warm days are a treasured rarity in Michigan, and so we occasionally met with students outside to take advantage of favorable weather. Although the sunshine was sweet that day, the material that we were told to study with the students, which came from then pastor Mark Driscoll of Mars Hill Church,[1] cast a shadow over our discussion, one that was palpable to the women and even some of the men. A rather controversial and inflammatory preacher, Driscoll once remarked that godly men in the Bible were "heterosexual, win-a-fight, punch-you-in-the-nose, dudes."[2] Two things in particular stood out from the study materials. First, "biblical manhood" was described in terms that seemed to bear a striking resemblance to what others might call "machismo," the stuff of John Wayne films and George C. Scott in the movie *Patton*. In terms of leadership—the purview of men alone—godly leaders are not "emotional" or "feminine." Second, "biblical womanhood" had a bizarre meaning. Definitionally, womanhood was described not in terms of what womanhood *is*, but in terms of what manhood *is not*. In other words, whereas manhood was clearly defined in positive terms, womanhood was vaguely defined merely by exclusion. Men were strongly encouraged to avoid looking anything like women, and women were warned not to act or behave in a disrespectful manner that could be perceived as masculine.

The lesson was striking, and its personal implications were profound. Even though I was a mentor to these students, and was not totally unfamiliar with such concepts, I myself came away wondering about my supposed place in the church. I had never before heard my gender, my role, and seemingly even my value to the church's mission described in such blunt and forceful terms. The experience made quite an impact on me, resulting in years of personal study and a quest for truth that culminated in this book.

As I soon discovered after beginning my journey, with respect to the issue of women in ministry, there is actually a broad spectrum of views within the evangelical world. However, like many spectrums, there are two predominant views. On one end is a position known as "complementarianism." In general terms, complementarians believe that it's God's unchanging design for men and women to fulfill different roles in relation to one another based on the permanent facts of creation. On the other end is a position known as "egalitarianism." In general terms, egalitarians take a contrary position and deny that there is any created or God-ordained hierarchy within the church based solely on gender. Fundamentally, the debate between complementarians and egalitarians is one of *gender-based line drawing*, particularly with regard to women in ministry.

Practically speaking, complementarians typically hold that certain offices (e.g., elder), ministries, and opportunities should, as a matter of biblical obedience and wisdom, be denied to women by virtue of their gender, regardless of personal gifting. Egalitarians, in contrast, place no restrictions based on gender in the local church structure. It's important to understand that these are just generalizations, and necessarily so. For example, complementarianism takes many forms, and its adherents in the academic literature offer different definitions and draw the lines in different places. More "conservative" complementarians would object to women assuming *any* formal teaching role within the local church, while more "centrist" complementarians likely would not. Given the many roles and functions within a local church, the lines must be drawn in many places (or not at all), and the variations are therefore numerous. While the terms "complementarian" and "egalitarian" can independently provoke positive or negative feelings on their own, throughout this book I have done my best to use the terms with which each side would self-identify so as not to shade them with my own bias.

Understandably, this debate has garnered much attention from academics, and since we'll be meeting them along the way, it seems best to introduce some of them now. As it turns out, there are highly educated, Greek-literate advocates on *both* sides of this issue.

Two of the most prominent advocates of what I call the "conservative" complementarian position are pastor John Piper and theologian Wayne Grudem. Their book *Recovering Biblical Manhood and Womanhood* can rightly be seen as conservative complementarians' most definitive defense. These two scholars were also instrumental in formulating the Danvers Statement[3] and forming the Council on Biblical Manhood and Womanhood. Piper summarizes their position in the following manner:

> When the Bible teaches that men and women fulfill different roles in relation to each other, charging man with a unique relationship role, it bases this differentiation not on temporary culture norms but on permanent facts of creation. This is seen in 1 Corinthians 11:3–16 (especially vv. 8–9, 14); Ephesians 5:21–33 (especially vv. 31–32);

and 1 Timothy 2:11–14 (especially vv. 13–14). In the Bible, differentiated roles for men and women . . . were corrupted, not created, by the fall. They were created by God.[4]

This view doesn't directly mention the ministry roles of women because it views all gender roles to be God-sanctioned through the original creative act and unchangeable regardless of the setting, whether the local church or marriage or the workplace. Elsewhere in their book, Piper further clarifies their position: "But we believe that manhood and womanhood mesh better in ministry when men take primary responsibility for leadership and teaching in the church; and that mature manhood and womanhood are better preserved, better nurtured, more fulfilled and more fruitful in this church order than in any other."[5] In this view, role distinctions are seen almost as the genetic inheritance from our first father and mother, and ultimately from God himself. Theologians Thomas Schreiner and Andreas Köstenberger are two other prominent members of this camp, and their book *Women in the Church* is another significant contribution to the debate from conservative complementarians.

The egalitarian position is best described by Rebecca Merrill Groothuis and Ronald Pierce in their book *Discovering Biblical Equality*:

> Biblical equality, therefore, denies that there is any created or otherwise God-ordained hierarchy *based solely on gender*. Egalitarianism recognizes patterns of authority in the family, church and society—it is not anachronistic—but rejects the notion that any office, ministry or opportunity should be denied anyone on the grounds of gender alone.[6]

This book contains a number of helpful essays from egalitarian scholars who offer a robust and well-researched counter-perspective to conservative complementarians.

There are also other voices that advocate for a middle ground. In *Neither Complementarian nor Egalitarian*, Michelle Lee-Barnewall aims to reframe the scholarly debate by emphasizing a servant leadership and kingdom mentality. She is an accomplished academic in her own right and adds a very interesting dynamic to the conversation; however, she intentionally stays away from the practical side of the discussion. Sarah Sumner is another academic who seeks a middle ground, and in *Men and Women in the Church* she advocates for qualified women to teach with the support of their congregation. Sumner also doesn't seem to fully self-identify with either the complementarian or egalitarian position, as she proposes a way forward within existing church structures.

At this point, you may be wondering why this debate even matters. And shouldn't I just get back to cooking dinner already? Before I burn the pot roast (I'm also English so boiling meat is almost a national pastime), please let me explain. Years ago, once my husband and I had taken on the challenge of navigating through the multitude of local church denominations, we finally settled on a church home. Selecting a local church sometimes involves a wide array of theological topics that require sorting through, but given my background I was quite unfamiliar with this debate regarding the role of women in a church community. And I suspect that I'm not alone in this. If a woman belongs to a local church community other than a purely egalitarian one—which I believe is true in most cases since egalitarian churches are in the minority—she has likely encountered various and possibly unspoken restrictions on roles for her female kind. This can be painful, confusing, and deeply frustrating for some.

But that's not why I've written this book. The purpose of this humble tome is not to settle the egalitarian and complementarian debate. Such a task is far beyond my little, gray, PhD-less brain cells. Nor is it to vent some form of deep-seated emotional hurt, either on behalf of myself or women in general. Rather, I carefully researched this topic for years and wrote this book with four clear purposes in mind.

First, I want to explain both the existence and the crux of the complementarian-egalitarian debate to other non-academics like myself. While many women are impacted by the practical outworking of this debate, it's quite understandable that few have the time (or interest) to read the dozens of academic books and articles that have already been written on this issue. My inspiration here is Shakespeare's character Polonius in *Hamlet*, whom I paraphrase: "The soul of wit is brevity, therefore I'll be brief."[7] In other words, this is intended as a brief guide to the major destination points along this journey (I considered trying to publish this book as part of the *Idiot's Guide* series, but sadly they have not yet decided to tackle issues such as this).

Second, I hope to add some levity to the discussion. As far as academic subjects go, this debate can be either heated or incredibly dry at times. Perhaps some humor is a needed remedy.

Third, in studying the debate in detail, I have noticed various fallacies, inconsistencies, and theologically unwarranted (or uncharitable) statements, especially from one camp in particular. To borrow a poker phrase, certain individuals might be "overplaying their hands," relying on questionable arguments or rhetoric to make their case. Behavior like this is worth noting and addressing, since it comes from some of the acknowledged "thought leaders" in this field.[8]

Finally, my intent is to explore the ways in which gifted

women—and Scripture declares that we all have gifts (1 Cor. 12:7)—can explore and develop their gifts in a non-confrontational, charitable fashion.[9] This was my challenge, and I want to impart the lessons that I've learned over the years.

Several other important points should be mentioned. First, no attack or criticism is in any way aimed towards the roles of homemaking or motherhood. I'm both a part-time homemaker and a mother, and these noble roles are certainly purposeful and joyous in their own right. For many women, though, these roles are not a part of their current life. Since the wife can become a widow, the child will grow into adulthood, and the gift of singleness may be non-returnable, I believe we all need to develop our minds and hearts—no matter the season or circumstances of life.

Second, these issues are relevant for anyone who is attending a complementarian local church, working or partnering with a complementarian parachurch ministry, or endeavoring to strike the right balance between the two predominant views on this topic. However, even if you attend an egalitarian church, I hope this information will serve to help you (or someone you care about) navigate this topic when it arises.

Finally, there are some followers of Christ who would not encourage others to read anything besides Scripture in seeking to understand or resolve this issue. While there is certainly great wisdom in studying the Bible for answers, the debate has escalated into a full-fledged theology of gender that might now have moved beyond what is written (1 Cor. 4:6). Such a development warrants careful evaluation. Again, I don't propose to settle the debate for you, dear reader, just to challenge you to engage with Scripture, inform you of the latest scholarship, and encourage you to be a seeker of truth through God's grace, just as you would in any other area of your faith.

In the interest of full disclosure, my own personal view is

somewhere in the middle of the spectrum, falling between the lines of a "liberal" complementarian and a cautious egalitarian. I have no problem acknowledging that my own bias from my childhood years as a Roman Catholic makes it difficult for me to ever accept a woman as the primary leader of a faith community. Even though I have participated in churches ranging from Baptist to Pentecostal, it's still difficult at times to see past the perspective shaped by my formative years. However, I have done my best to remain objective by studying the academic work published by *both* sides of the debate. What follows is a non-academic, layman's journey into the world of scholarship to discover some simple truths regarding the way forward.

With that said, let us turn now to the key factors that impact the debate before a single verse is read—namely, grammar, culture, and bias. Although a reader may not initially notice these influences, they can subtly shape our conclusions and impact our lives in astounding ways.

CHAPTER 2

Grammar, Culture, and Bias: Unavoidable Factors that Shape the Gender Debate

> Trust not yourself; but your defects to know,
> Make use of ev'ry friend—and ev'ry foe.
>
> —Alexander Pope, "An Essay on Criticism"

> But who can discern their own errors?
>   Forgive my hidden faults.
> Keep your servant also from willful sins;
>   may they not rule over me.
>
> —Psalm 19:12–13

THE YOUNG COLLEGE student dashed out of the lecture hall. Although the speaker's message at the weekly college ministry meeting was still in full swing, he needed to exit the room immediately. The reason for his hasty departure was simple: the person giving the message was a *woman*.

The student, with anger and frustration visibly rising, paced back and forth outside the room. He told me and others who came to check on him that he wouldn't stand for it. He was going to... write a letter to the parachurch organization that was behind the dastardly meeting! He declared that he was a man and should *not* be taught by a woman in any capacity. It would be perfectly fine if this were a youth class or children's Sunday school class, but he was no longer a boy and shouldn't be asked to sit and listen to a teaching on Scripture unless a *man* was doing the teaching.

At this time I had only been a committed follower of Jesus for a few months, and I found this entire scene to be more than a little perplexing. Once I realized that this friend had not hurriedly left the room because of a dire family crisis or a severe gastrological complaint, I was really at a loss as to why this was such a big deal. Having been raised Roman Catholic, I was very familiar with the rule of men—and men alone—serving in a leader's teaching role at church. But we weren't in a local church. We were in a secular university lecture hall with gum under the desks and none of the usual markings of a church such as baptism, communion, or a congregation of members.

After the student had calmed down somewhat, he and I talked about the Bible verses in 1 Timothy 2 and 1 Corinthians 14, which showed, at least in his mind, why he shouldn't be subjected to a female teacher on spiritual issues. He said that he was being faithful to his reading of Scripture and true to his own conscience. As for me, this was an eye-opening experience and my first encounter with the difficulties and consequences of interpreting the Scripture passages affecting the role of women in the church.

As far as I can tell, passages like 1 Timothy 2:9–15 and 1

Corinthians 14 are so hotly debated because of three factors: (1) sparse or complex grammatical evidence; (2) varying levels of reliance upon Greco-Roman culture in biblical interpretation; and (3) the interpreter's personal lens, sometimes also referred to as "bias" or "horizon."[1] Some further comments about each factor are in order.

A Matter of Words: Grammar

I mentioned previously that the debate between complementarians and egalitarians is fundamentally one of line drawing, particularly with regard to women in ministry. But this prompts another question: On what basis are the lines drawn in the first place? Why would anyone in a local church conclude that *gender* is a legitimate basis upon which to exclude or prevent an entire group of people (i.e., women) from serving in certain roles or utilizing certain gifts in particular settings?

At its very core, the debate primarily turns on Paul's intended meaning in 1 Timothy 2:19–15 and especially over a particular word in the passage. The key portion of this passage reads as follows: "I do not permit a woman to teach or to assume authority [*authenteō*] over a man; she must be quiet. For Adam was formed first, then Eve. And Adam was not the one deceived; it was the woman who was deceived and became a sinner."[2] The meaning of this single Greek word *authenteō* is very important, and it's no stretch to claim that this entire passage is central to the debate. To see this, one only has to note that the book *Women in the Church*, written by conservative complementarians Andreas Köstenberger and Thomas Schreiner, deals solely with 1 Timothy 2:9–15, is in its third printing, and runs to more than 340 pages in length. In addition, the book's *bibliography* is over thirty pages long, revealing just how much attention this issue has received from theologians and other academics. The amount of ink devoted to these seven verses demonstrates their importance.

Secondarily, the debate involves the meaning of two other words in the Bible. The first is the meaning of ᶜēzer, often translated as "helper" in Genesis 2. For example, God concluded that it "is not good for the man to be alone. I will make a helper [ᶜēzer] suitable for him" (Gen. 2:18). The second is the meaning of *kephalē* in passages such as 1 Corinthians 11:1–10. For example, Paul writes that "I want you to realize that the head of every man is Christ, and the head [*kephalē*] of the woman is man, and the head of Christ is God" (1 Cor. 11:3).

Other words and passages are debated as well, but these are all less relevant in nature compared to the passages cited above. Ultimately, the debate focuses on what the apostle Paul meant nearly two thousand years ago when he penned a short letter to his young protégé who was in need of support and encouragement as he ministered to the fledgling church in Ephesus (1 Tim. 1:3; 4:12).

At this point, you may be asking yourself a very reasonable question: Why is a high-level academic debate about *grammar* so complicated and divisive? We never hear about Scrabble players getting into fistfights or crossword enthusiasts meeting with pistols at dawn. How can there be such disagreement over the meaning of *three words*—*authenteō*, ᶜēzer, and *kephalē*—to the extent that it directly impacts women who have never set foot in the halls of Christian academia?

The phrase "it's all Greek to me" is attributed to Shakespeare's play *Julius Caesar*. And for the average Christian, the phrase is entirely appropriate, because virtually no one studies Greek anymore. However, even for the academics who participate in this debate—all of whom are Greek scholars in the sense that they have a solid understanding of biblical Greek—the ancient language is still quite complex and heavily reliant upon context to determine meaning. For example, Greek is an *inflected* language. This means that verbs and nouns have what is referred to as a "stem" that doesn't change and an ending that is customized to fit the context. In other words, the ending of a verb or noun conveys crucial information, telling the reader which one of four (or sometimes five) cases[3] applies and therefore how the persons, objects, and actions are all related. I'm greatly simplifying things for the sake of brevity, but the point is that word meaning is heavily dependent upon the content *and* context of the passage at hand. Moreover, when translating from Greek to English, deciding which word is the best contextual fit for a given passage is an issue on which many educated, godly teachers can and often do disagree. I will have much more to say about exegesis[4] of the key passages in chapter 5. At this point, however, I just want to point out that grammar—how we use, understand, and translate a word—has a huge effect on this debate.

The Times, They Are a Changing: Culture

Regarding biblical interpretation, our modern world is vastly changed from the Greco-Roman world of the first century when the inspired words of the New Testament were composed. Moreover, the impact of that change is far deeper than just a cultural move away from head coverings as a fashion statement of modesty (1 Cor. 11:4–6) or a greeting marked by a "holy kiss" (Rom. 16:16; 2 Cor. 13:12). During this period in history, the education of most girls was suspended at roughly age fourteen, when they were usually married off to a man roughly ten years or more their senior.[5] Men, on the other hand, were educated until much later in life and had more personal freedoms than their female counterparts. Not only that, but the Aristotelian view prevalent in the Greco-Roman world was that women were less able to learn than men and on the whole women were not very rational beings.⁶ The local church itself looked almost nothing like the churches that most of us attend today. Many were operated within an individual's home with likely only a small group of people and a local elder who would shepherd and oversee the group. There was nothing close to the level of structure that characterizes most evangelical churches today.

Michelle Lee-Barnewall offers an interesting history of the many ways that women were actively involved in preaching and teaching ministries throughout the history of the church, both in mission fields and on home soil. It was only in the aftermath of the World Wars, when the domestic family unit became elevated to the point that the national role of women shifted to full-time homemakers, that this acceptance was rolled back and women ceased to function as front-line missionaries.⁷ Cultural roles of women have changed over time, and this too has affected how women are viewed in the church.

One local church I attended was ardently complementarian to the point that an individual woman was not permitted to lead a co-ed small group Bible study without a male co-leader present, in honor of 1 Timothy 2:12. Theologically, the members of this community would never contend that women are worth any less than men or that women are not also marked by the *Imago Dei* (Gen. 1:27). However, gifted, well-educated, and biblically literate women could reasonably infer as much from this sort of practice. As egalitarian Walter Liefeld observes:

> Plutarch, who lived in apostolic times, said that it was equally shameful for a woman to speak in public and to have a bare arm. We need to realize that in Paul's day a woman's speaking and teaching in the church could

constitute a moral problem and bring shame on the church and on the Lord, thus keeping people from Christ. That is simply not true in most societies today, at least in the Western world. In fact, the situation is reversed: to prohibit a woman from having the same dignity and opportunity in church as she does in society is a stumbling block to many people. Therefore, by earnestly trying to make the same application (the silence of women) rather than following the same principle (avoiding shame and dishonor to the husband), we can actually commit the very error Paul sought to avoid—that is, offending people's moral sensibilities and hindering them from accepting the gospel.[8]

This quote from Liefeld highlights something important: how we view our culture also affects how we interpret the Bible.

Conservative complementarian Thomas Schreiner offers his own interesting method of biblical interpretation: "Increasingly, being a Bible-believing Christian in this world—or taking one's cue from Scripture alone—means swimming upstream and being countercultural."[9] This is an assumption that seems to be shared by many conservative complementarians. Specifically, they argue that the more countercultural reading of Scripture is likely to be the correct one.[10] Now, I'm certainly not denying that the gospel itself is countercultural. The life of Jesus was *radically* countercultural, in part because it involved the arrival of an upside-down kingdom in which the strong were called to surrender power in order to elevate the weak. To see this, look no further than the Sermon on the Mount.[11] However, what is true with respect to societal structures is not necessarily true with respect to hermeneutics, or the science of biblical interpretation. While Jesus called us to *live* counterculturally—to seek first his kingdom and righteousness

(Matt. 6:33)—there is no similar call to *interpret* counterculturally. As complementarian Craig Blomberg explains, "We need to comprehend the *perspective* of the original communicators—author and readers—to understand the correct meaning."[12] In other words, the meaning of a biblical text is heavily informed by the culture in which it was originally situated, not by a contrary position to our modern culture. Paul certainly seemed to take culture into account as he moved from city to city and became all things to all people (1 Cor. 9:22).

Some complementarians charge egalitarians with gleaning influences from modern culture and feminism. After being accused of conforming to the secular culture instead of remaining faithful to Scripture, egalitarians are discounted merely on these grounds alone. But if even the most conservative complementarians are permitted to launch their theological crusade as a reaction to modern-day culture, then surely egalitarians are equally free to appeal to culture—specifically the Greco-Roman culture that Paul inhabited—in defending their position. Otherwise, it's difficult to avoid the conclusion that these complementarians are engaging in special pleading, which is nothing more than a logical fallacy.

All this to say that our stance toward culture—both ancient culture and current day culture—has a heavy bearing on how we interpret Scripture in this debate.

The View from My Seat: Bias

Finally, no one approaches this topic without a bias, a lens or way of viewing the world based upon past experiences (both positive and negative), and a family culture that influenced one's earliest thoughts on roles and gender. For example, a modern, secular, educated woman who is raised to believe that she can do anything a man can do might view the restrictions on women in church ministry as bewildering and hurtful at best, and as sexist and discriminatory at worst. Meanwhile, a woman raised in a loving Christian family and nurturing conservative church may more readily accept and even in some ways have learned to appreciate traditional gender roles in the church. My college friend who fled the campus ministry meeting like a house on fire was raised in a strong Baptist tradition that confined women in the church to teaching small children or other women. When he encountered a woman teaching adults of *both* genders, all this Baptist young man could think to do in the moment was to flee as if some strange religious practice had just begun that involved dancing, singing, or clapping on the downbeat.

I will admit that in my own case, even after carefully identifying my personal bias, it can still be challenging to navigate this topic with clarity and without the pitfalls of past hurts or perceived "rights." When I began researching this issue over six years ago, I was initially under the impression that discovering the answers to these questions would involve only a few months of intensive reading and reflection, but here I am at least a dozen academic-level books later and the issue is still one that can be staggeringly complex. Even so, I believe that any woman earnestly wrestling with this issue should take heart. Study of this topic may not crystallize an answer that is one hundred percent certain; sometimes in this life we will only know in part (1 Cor. 13:12). However, there is sufficient information and accessible scholarship on the relevant issues to enable a motivated individual to reach a practical resolution that honors both Scripture and the desire to maximize the use of her personal gifts.

When all is said and done, the key to studying this topic is to be open to studying the issue, and to humbly realize that the issues are complex, we lack perfect knowledge, and even the knowledge we have is shaped by our own culture and biases. In other words, the complexity of the biblical data is such that a person from either side of the debate could be in the wrong.[13] Grammar, culture, and bias are all unavoidable factors, and whether we like it or not, they shape our thoughts and lives—and this often thorny debate.

CHAPTER 3

Are Women Inferior? Sexism in History, Theology, and Practice

The paramount destiny and mission of woman are to fulfill the noble and benign offices of wife and mother. This is the law of the Creator.

—*Bradwell v. Illinois* (1873)

A woman, especially, if she has the misfortune of knowing anything, should conceal it as well as she can.

—Jane Austen, *Northanger Abbey*

"Women don't need a watch; there's a clock on the oven!" I often heard this joke during my adolescence, as it was a favorite one-liner of my male family members. As the target of this joke, I found it surprising at first, then even a bit funny, and then just tired in the end.

Unfortunately, this wouldn't be my last experience with

sexism. Over the past ten years I have worked in the male-dominated financial services industry as a compliance officer. As tax collectors were in the first century to their fellow Jewish countrymen, so compliance officers are today to others in the financial services industry. At conferences, I have actually experienced people choosing *not* to sit near me upon learning my job title. Such a reaction is not uncommon. For many years, I was tasked with reviewing the "suitability" of customer sales, and this often placed me directly between a financial advisor and his impending sales commission. As anyone who has endured this role can tell you, the "sales reviewer" chair is rarely a comfortable or cozy place to sit. The difficulty of my role was heightened by the fact that most of the sales reps were older men who had been in the industry for decades, a fact that they often shared during confrontational phone calls. The number of times that I was called "honey," "sweetie," or "darling" in the middle of discussing a sales review was staggering. While not all of the calls were combative, and many men were very respectful and appreciative of my efforts to keep them out of regulators' crosshairs, whenever conflict did arise, my male colleagues didn't experience the same tone and language that were exhibited towards me. It was almost as though advisors believed that if they were firm and masculine enough in their demeanor, they could get me to change my mind about rejecting or questioning the appropriateness of their investment recommendation.

Sexism in History and Theology

Now, you may be wondering what a secular job in finance has to do with the topic at hand. Has this author had so many cups of tea today that the tannin is causing mental lapses? Almost certainly yes, but the reason that I share this story is because

Aristotle is still holding court in the twenty-first century. You may not think that this philosopher of old continues to exert as much influence as he once did, especially since he is long dead, but his teaching on the intrinsic *inferiority* of women is still alive and well today. For example, consider this ancient gem of Aristotelian wisdom: "[A]s between the sexes, the male is by nature superior and the female inferior, the male ruler and the female subject."[1] From my interaction with certain financial advisors, one would be tempted to think that studying Aristotle was part of their training.

Aristotle is by no means the only voice from antiquity to express such views. In fact, many of the church fathers and theologians of old were influenced by these sentiments to some degree. While many examples could be cited, the following sufficiently illustrate the point:

> **Tertullian**: "You are the devil's gateway; you are she who first violated the forbidden tree and broke the law of God. It was you who coaxed your way around him whom the devil had not the force to attack. With what ease you shattered that image of God: man! Because of the death you merited, the Son of God had to die."[2]

> **Augustine**: "The woman herself alone is not the image of God: whereas the man alone is the image of God as fully and completely as when the woman is joined with him."[3]

> **Aquinas**: "As regards the individual nature, woman is defective and misbegotten, for the active force in the male seed tends to the production of a perfect likeness in the masculine sex; while the production of women comes from a defect in the active force or from some material indisposition or even from some external influence."[4]

Aristotle's robe and hairstyle might be a faux pas these days (unless you're a Greek tour guide), but his assumptions about women are not. This tradition is still part of the workplace experience for many women, even if only in subtle forms.

Sexism in Practice

As I began to research the different views on women in ministry, I was aghast to learn that John Piper, one of the leading voices among conservative complementarians, has actually asserted that my job as a compliance officer is in *violation* of God's plans for biblical womanhood. Specifically, because my role—which is one of authority—is at times both personal and directive, it could be seen to "offend a man's good, God-given sense of responsibility and leadership, and thus controvert God's created order."[5] Now, in the more disagreeable instances, my role really just offended the advisor's pocketbook, since he could not receive his sales commission unless I approved his sale for processing. But quitting my job, as much as I may have wished to do so, was for many years never an option. My husband was a full-time law student and we relied upon my income for support. The only option open to me in this season was to navigate the job to the best of my ability and find a way to communicate the bad news of sales rejections in a manner that was as friendly as possible.

However, if there are also a number of secular (i.e., non-ministry) employment positions that I shouldn't hold simply because of my easily deceived, weaker-armed gender, then the most conservative form of complementarianism seems to be almost impossible for women to practically live out (the weakness of women's arms was noted as a failing of our gender by the character Dwight Schrute in *The Office*). If avoiding the possibility of "offending" male sensibilities is paramount and necessary in order to avoid fouling up God's orderly universe, as Piper suggests it is, then employment opportunities for women must necessarily be quite limited. According to Piper, there are certain professions that women shouldn't pursue, including judge, police officer, legislator, college teacher, and school principal.[6]

Although it may seem like I'm trying to attack one side, this is honestly not my intent. Really, my purposes are twofold. First, I believe that we need to combat any unhealthy or unbiblical view of women. To do so is not "evangelical feminism"; rather, it's biblical. Piper and Grudem have had much to say in response to "evangelical feminism," but it's not a feminist statement to insist that women in the church not be regarded as intellectually inferior to men. But sadly, what I experienced in my secular profession is common within the church as well. Sarah Sumner holds a PhD from a prestigious seminary and is herself an accomplished academic who serves as the dean of a seminary in California. She notes the assumptions—rooted in historical theology—that still pervade the church today:

> If church tradition was based on Scripture, then so be it. But church tradition regarding women is based on the church fathers' belief that women are inferior to men.... Indeed, Christians in the past did not stand up and say, "Women are men's equals, but God says to prohibit them anyway." They said, "God said women are to be prohibited precisely because women are inferior."[7]

Here Sumner is highlighting the historical fact that the notion of women having "equal value" but different roles (roles will be discussed in more detail in a later chapter) is a *new* addition to an old debate. For many years, as the church father quotes show, some traditions within the church were supportive of this idea that women are the weaker gender in more than just the sense of physical fitness (1 Peter 3:7).

Second, I want to highlight just how damaging such assumptions are to the church and the gospel message with which it has been entrusted. Jesus came to give us eternal and abundant life (John 10:10). When we don't encourage women to learn, grow, and serve with their gifts as much as possible, nonbelievers have a hard time differentiating between the supposedly radical message of the Christian gospel and the broken world around us that in many ways still rejoices more when one son is born than any number of daughters. Blomberg is candid about this issue:

> Even in an increasingly egalitarian secular world, women are taken advantage of in hurtful ways far more often than men, in situations that largely remain outside their control. The church should be known as a refuge against such behavior; tragically, it often perpetrates it, at times even more than in the outside world.[8]

It's hopefully an extremely rare occurrence that a Christian church would value women any less than men, as doing so would be a direct contradiction of the gospel which asserts that men and women are equal in Christ Jesus (Gal. 3:28). However, when a church expends great amounts of energy to invest in male leadership while simultaneously restricting or limiting the roles of women, the emotional toll on women can be quite high. When the gender roles of a church are so important that they are placed just a few steps below (or on par with) the gospel itself, many women may have a difficult time seeing the joy and hope of Jesus in spite of these barriers.

Some might object that to reason in such a manner is to commit a logical fallacy. Specifically, some might infer that

I'm insisting that complementarianism is false because of the emotional impact it may have on women. While that *would* be a logical fallacy, that is not my position. Like any position, complementarianism stands or falls based on the textual evidence and arguments in its favor. In other words, complementarianism cannot be refuted based upon the *feelings* that it creates in others, particularly women, no more than egalitarianism can be refuted based upon the feelings it creates in men. However, the consequences which follow from the more conservative form of complementarianism (à la Piper or Schreiner) are not insignificant. Indeed, if the consequences of conservative complementarianism can be shown to strongly conflict with other clear biblical principles, then the doctrine of inerrancy—that Scripture is without error—would suggest that the position of conservative complementarianism is itself unbiblical.

Theology and the Abuse of Power

In the fall of 2017, a name from the production halls of Hollywood burst onto the news scene in a very shocking and lasting way: Harvey Weinstein. The accusations of sexual harassment against Weinstein (and many others in his industry) have made him an infamous household name, even to people like me who don't watch many movies. While such abusive behavior has probably always occurred, these public disclosures have revealed just how common such behavior remains throughout American society, even in our supposedly enlightened times. Truly, there is nothing new under the sun (Eccl. 1:9).

Unfortunately, the behavior of Weinstein and his ilk is not limited to an industry known for idolizing and portraying sexuality in a graphic manner. Evangelicals have also seen fallout from the #MeToo movement, with the exposure of everything from crude jokes to predatory behavior to spiritual abuse in a wide variety of churches and denominations.

It shouldn't need to be said, but God doesn't tolerate any abuse that involves wielding a position of power or strength to prey upon another human being in a position of weakness or vulnerability (Mark 10:42–45). In addition, Scripture is clear that the sexual behavior of believers is to be above reproach (Eph 5:3), and that leaders of the church are especially charged not to lord it over their flock, but to be examples to them of godliness and love (1 Pet. 5:3).

The failure of men to remain sexually pure and to carry out what complementarians perceive as their God-ordained role to lead and protect women doesn't disprove their argument, but it does serve to highlight the many ways in which women still live in vulnerable and powerless situations. Does the church succeed in countering the notion, from nearly every patriarchal culture that has existed on this earth, that women are less? We know from the Gospels that Jesus himself countered these notions in a radical way, but has the church continued to do so?

In the early church, women were welcomed and even celebrated. Jesus chose to be born of a woman. He accepted the financial and personal support of women (Luke 8:3), encouraged women to sit at his feet and learn from him (Luke 10:38–42), talked to a disgraced woman as though she were his full intellectual and gender equal (John 4:1–42), and revealed himself to women after his resurrection[9] (John 20:10–18). Later, women hosted churches, carried out compassionate charity, and labored side by side with Paul (Acts 16:14, 40). And as the influence of Christianity spread, abortion rates for females fell, men were drawn into the church by their godly wives, and marriages became not just economic institutions but covenants of love. As a result, the church grew and spread.[10]

Of course this was the Wild West of Christianity, before overly formal structures, rules, and roles were born. When Emperor Constantine converted, he required the Christian structures to fit within the existing Roman ones. As historian and seminary professor Bruce Shelley notes, "Constantine ruled Christian bishops as he did his civil servants and demanded unconditional obedience to official pronouncements, even when they interfered with purely church matters.... Prior to Constantine's conversion, the church consisted of convinced believers. Now many came who were politically ambitious, religiously disinterested, and still half-rooted in paganism."[11] The medieval church also reintroduced Hebrew purity laws which cemented the exclusion of people who have that problem of being "unclean" each month for several days.[12] And ever since then, culture has influenced the church as much, if not more, than the church has influenced culture.

You Run Like a Girl

As a child (or even as an adult), there are few things worse or more embarrassing for a boy than losing to a girl. Whether it involves a playground game of four-square or a spelling bee competition, the clamoring jeers and humiliation of "You got beat by a girl!" would sting deeply. Each year, several dozen members of my husband's maternal relatives gather for a week-long vacation near Lake Huron, and at some point during the trip an inevitable game of Trivial Pursuit occurs in which the men battle the women for trivia bragging rights. Without fail, the men always boast that they have "no weaknesses," which makes it all the more crushing for them when they lose.

Boys naturally compare themselves to girls. This is behavior we learn on the playground, and it carries over to adulthood. And since being equated to (or beaten by) a girl is anything but positive, this certainly doesn't paint women very favorably. Rather than just "You lost!" or "You didn't play up to your potential!" the *insult* is "You lost to a girl!"

In terms of how this relates to the church, consider what Piper says about how a "mature woman" will behave:

> [S]he will affirm and receive and nurture the strength and leadership of men *in some form* in all her relationships with men.... To the degree that a woman's influence over man is personal and directive it will generally offend a man's good, God-given sense of responsibility and leadership, and thus controvert God's created order.... The God-given sense of responsibility for leadership in a mature man will not generally allow him to flourish long under personal, directive leadership of a female superior.... I would stress that this is not necessarily owing to male egotism, but to a natural and good penchant given by God.[13]

Such an understanding of "mature" manhood and womanhood invites comparison. However, some participants in the debate argue that the *type* of comparison it invites can be rather unhealthy. As Sumner comments:

> [Piper's] objective, I believe, is to prompt Christian men to be responsible. "At the heart of mature masculinity," he says, "is a sense of benevolent responsibility to lead, provide for and protect women." If all men everywhere adhered to this definition, the world would be a far better place.... But it wouldn't solve the issue. Instead, another problem would arise.... Though Piper's definition of manhood is congenial toward women, it fails women. It also inevitably fails men. Christian men are

continually being taught to measure themselves against women. . . . Piper's definition of mature manhood strikes an inner cord with men. It offers men a formula by which to identify themselves as men, not boys and not women. And yet . . . it teaches men to believe that manhood fundamentally is a feeling. Manhood, he says, is something a man senses within himself. If ever he doesn't sense it, he is led to believe it disappears.[14]

Notice once more what Piper says: "To the degree that a woman's influence over man is personal and directive it will generally offend a man's good, God-given sense of responsibility and leadership, and thus controvert God's created order." In other words, men have every reason to feel and act like responsible leaders, but when women "offend" this sensibility it *violates the natural order of things*. Moreover, men have every right to be offended: "I would stress that this is not necessarily owing to male egotism, but to a natural and good penchant given by God." Stated differently, the "penchant" for being offended is not due to male pride but was placed there by God, so by all means don't dare offend!

But can we really say that *none* of this "offense" is due to pride? If the human heart "is deceitful above all things" (Jer. 17:9), how confident can anyone be that "male egotism" is no part of the equation? Not only does Piper fail to cite a Bible verse in support of his claims (even though other claims on the same page of his book receive a Scripture citation), he also seems to underestimate the subtlety of pride. In the book *Respectable Sins*, author Jerry Bridges observes that the sin of pride can take several different forms, including "moral self-righteousness" and "correct doctrine."[15] The latter manifests itself when a person thinks that his belief system is superior to others, while failing to treat others with respect or realize that godly scholars may hold differing beliefs for legitimate reasons.[16] Because the sin of pride is subtle, it's not an *ad hominem* or personal attack to ask whether some conservative complementarians *may* have unwittingly fallen prey to it.

Therefore, if pride is really behind some complementarian theology, what is motivating this pride? One possibility is suggested by C. S. Lewis: "Now what you want to get clear is that Pride is essentially competitive—is competitive by its very nature—while the other vices are competitive only, so to speak, by accident."[17] Philosopher and theologian William Lane Craig has remarked that "female philosophers and especially Christian female philosophers are a tiny minority" in academia, as are female theologians and female historical Jesus scholars—although we need more of all of them.[18] It's not inconceivable that, at some unconscious level, certain members of this mostly male club may prefer things that way. But if we are indeed a body of Christ made up of many different parts, then how could any gift in another person be discouraged? When attempts are made to curtail women's roles or limit the exercise of their gifts, one can never completely rule out the possibility that a pricked pride, jealousy, or insecurity could be at the root of some (or all) of it.

It's certainly true that we should "clothe [our]selves with humility toward one another, because, 'God opposes the proud but shows favor to the humble'" (1 Pet. 5:5). And no doubt both genders exhibit pride in certain areas of life or at certain times.[19] Competitiveness and comparison are not necessarily more prevalent in one gender over the other. While one can see how it's natural for men to be more physically competitive given their greater size and strength, why does this seem to spill over to other areas as well? It's not an uncommon experience for women in the church to be gently "encouraged" to hold back, act in a "quiet" manner, or help out with more "traditional" roles such as the latest bake sale. Now, I'm all for bake sales, especially if there's a quality English breakfast tea on hand to accompany the cakes and pies.[20] But the point is this: If there is an inability (or an unwillingness) to encourage the gifts that are clearly seen in brothers *and* sisters in Christ, then we are in an important sense rejecting part of the body—the church—and telling that part that its gifts are unnecessary or less important.[21] The result is an inability to celebrate or to "rejoice with those who rejoice" (Rom. 12:15) when their gifts are identified and developed for the glory of God.

CHAPTER 4

Rising Tensions: A Secondary Doctrine No Longer

Fallacies do not cease to be fallacies because they become fashions.

—G. K. Chesterton, *Napoleon of Notting Hill*

*B*ANG! A strange noise erupted under our car. It was the late 1980s, and my mother, father, older brother, and I were driving through the streets of Detroit. Although I was only five years old, the strange noise and the debate that followed between my parents terrified me. My mother screamed, "You've been shot!" My father replied with a calm, "No, no, it was just a thrown rod. I'll pull over and check it out." This debate continued for several minutes until the dome light came on to reveal that while the car had a problem, it was now most certainly the less important one. The splatter of red inside the car confirmed that my father had indeed been shot in the foot. I later learned that the noise we heard was the bullet entering the car and then passing though his foot before landing on the floor by our feet.

Though he couldn't see it in the moment, my father's first response was to elevate fixing the car above saving his own life. Thankfully, my mother was able to help him to the passenger seat and drive him to the nearest hospital for immediate treatment. He suffered a broken bone and bullet fragment damage, but considering what could have been, we were very thankful to all be alive.

Additions to "Core Values"

Since the gospel is the very hope of life, isn't it imperative not to include any non-essentials with that message? The apostle Paul certainly thought so: "But even if we or an angel from heaven should preach a gospel other than the one we preached to you, let them be under God's curse!" (Gal. 1:8). And again: "For I resolved to know nothing while I was with you except Jesus Christ and him crucified" (1 Cor. 2:2). If my father had insisted on calling a tow truck or getting a car wash after he had been shot, we would have wondered about his sanity. When the stakes are high, there's only time for that which is essential to safety and survival. Those things which are non-essential cannot be elevated to a place of highest importance when they get in the way of, or distract from, what really matters. Unfortunately, in more recent years, a number of local churches seem to have forgotten this important lesson when it comes to the gospel message.

Local churches are run by pastors who shape church policy, and pastors in turn are shaped by the theologians who mold and instruct them over a period of several intense years of study. In short, the academic complementarian-egalitarian debate reaches the average local church attendee through human conduits: pastors. However, this hasn't been without consequences. Paul's unadorned gospel message—a core truth of the Christian faith—now finds itself in the strange company of a "new" core value: complementarianism. Certain complementarian theologians have elevated what is arguably a secondary or tertiary doctrine into a matter of primary importance, and pastors have taken notice. Some ministries now include their stance on this issue among their primary distinctives. For example, consider the Acts 29 church planting network. In the "What We Believe" section of its website, Acts 29 provides the following information:

> While we believe it is vital that the elders of each of our churches determine where they stand on doctrines of second importance, we do wish to make known our convictions on the following five theologically-driven core values: [1] Gospel centrality in all of life, [2] The sovereignty of God in saving sinners, [3] The work of the Holy Spirit for life and ministry, [4] The equality of male and female and the principle of male servant leadership, [5] The local church as God's primary mission strategy.[1]

Two things should be noted. First, the fourth item is an explicit endorsement of complementarianism, as suggested by the phrase "principle of male servant leadership."[2] Second, complementarianism has been elevated to a "core value" rather than a "doctrine of second importance," placed right alongside the gospel, God's sovereignty, and the empowerment of the Holy Spirit.[3] This seems deeply misguided.[4]

A recent article by Albert Mohler, one of the leaders within the prominent Southern Baptist Convention (SBC), is also worth mentioning. Mohler writes that:

> The SBC has affirmed complementarianism—the belief that the Bible reveals that men and women are equally made in God's image, but that men and women were also created to be complements to each other, men and women bearing distinct and different roles. This means obeying the Bible's very clear teachings on male leadership in the home and in the church. By the year 2000, complementarian teachings were formally included within the Baptist Faith & Message, the denomination's confession of faith.[5]

Mohler's article was prompted by recent scandals that have come to light within the leaderships ranks of the SBC, which is the largest Protestant denomination in America. Although Mohler offers a defense regarding why complementarian theology is not a part of the problem, the fact that SBC theology now includes complementarianism in its "confession of faith" *is* itself a rather big problem. (This is not to say that one denomination is guiltier of the sort of abuse that Mohler addresses, but rather to highlight the recent elevation to "statements of faith" taking place with respect to theology that has a direct bearing on church culture and the development of women's spiritual gifts.) Returning to the concept of the gospel's essential content, why would the roles of women in the local church need to be part of any confession of Christian faith? For example, what does this have to do with Jesus' death on the cross as our substitutionary atonement? While pastors have a legitimate practical need to navigate where they stand on the role of women serving in the local church, this non-essential doctrine lacks the weighty substance of an older statement of

Women's Gifts, Women's Roles 43

faith such as the Apostles Creed. In terms of running the SBC and the Acts 29 network, the wider impact on church culture and allocating resources is sure to be profound.

The rhetoric can run quite deeply on this issue, and two regrettable examples illustrate the point. First, consider a radical claim made in the preface to Piper and Grudem's book: "Egalitarianism must always lead to an eventual denial of the gospel."[6] I want you to read that sentence again. This is no less than a bold assertion that to disagree with the conservative complementarianism espoused by Piper and Grudem is to set off down the *inevitable* road to heresy. Even though I'm not arguing for egalitarianism here—just a defense for the development of women and their gifts—the spirit of division in such a comment simply doesn't foster unity or benefit the discussion. Indeed, the mind boggles at how someone with a doctorate could make such a statement. For it simply doesn't follow that egalitarianism "must always" lead to a "denial of the gospel." As a philosopher might say, the conclusion doesn't follow from the premises; in this case we have a clear *non sequitur*. As a counterexample, egalitarian Craig Keener is not only a gifted New Testament scholar, but his impressive work in Christian apologetics has helped many come to know Christ.[7] So much for egalitarianism leading people away from the gospel.

Biblical Fidelity on the Line

Second, consider this comment—from the chancellor of Reformed Theological Seminary—endorsing another Piper and Grudem book:

> At the core of this topic lies the fundamental issue of biblical authority. If we deny biblical teaching about

manhood and womanhood, the possibility of a definitive interpretation is lost. If we can get egalitarianism from the Bible, then we can read anything into it. Piper and Grudem's book dispels the confusion and points us back to biblical fidelity.[8]

Again, we have another astonishing rhetorical claim. In addition to heresy, egalitarianism also inevitably leads to false doctrine and eisegesis (that is, reading your own meaning into Scripture). Whether intended or not, such comments elevate Piper and Grudem (and other conservative complementarian scholars like them) to biblical gatekeepers, self-appointed watchdogs who insist that to deny their view of complementarianism is to take a headfirst leap down the Slip-'n'-Slide of destructive theology. What else besides something like heresy can be inferred from the stark words "pointing us back to biblical fidelity"?[9] The language of power now expressed regarding this topic is remarkable and, to this author, deeply troubling. However, these comments reflect the current climate that has seen this issue continue to increase in importance within many sects of the Protestant church in America, becoming ever more closely tied to orthodoxy itself. Though the Westminster Confession of Faith speaks not one word about gender roles,[10] egalitarianism or any challenge to the current establishment built upon the foundation of complementarian "role theology" is seen to be divisive and potentially dangerous. As a former Roman Catholic, I cannot help but be reminded of the many "anathemas" (i.e., forceful theological condemnations) that the Council of Trent issued in response to what it perceived to be the dangerous false teaching of the Reformation. Today, egalitarians risk their own anathemas from the Council on Biblical Manhood and Womanhood.

As the previous quotations demonstrate, the complementarian-egalitarian debate is no longer being treated as a "peripheral" issue in any sense. Instead, a reactionary approach to cultural shifts has elevated this issue from the pages of academic journals and books onto the lists of "distinctives" and "core values" adopted by many churches. Since this strain of conservative complementarianism is self-portrayed by its advocates as the sole (or at least the best) position that holds a "high view of Scripture," to disagree with their conclusions is to "go against Scripture" with "new" interpretations that wrongly allow culture to inform biblical interpretation.

But is this necessarily the case? As I've mentioned, my stated aim is not to attack complementarianism as a plausible position (which it is). Rather, I want the women (and men) in the local church to know that the debate isn't as settled or as much of a one-sided "slam-dunk" case as conservative complementarians make it out to be with their language of "biblical fidelity" and the like. In some instances, it seems that certain conservative complementarian leaders with power and influence have misused their authority and made unsubstantiated claims, committing logical fallacies, sowing division, and insinuating "biblical infidelity" towards others along the way. This simply will not do. By overplaying their hand, conservative complementarians have effectively committed the very act for which they often criticize their egalitarian opponents: going beyond what is written (1 Cor. 4:6). However, seeing why this is so requires a more in-depth understanding of what the debate is all about. Consequently, it's time to look to the biblical evidence itself. Dear reader, it's time to join me for what may seem like a strange exercise at first, but I promise will be a rewarding adventure of discovery, one that takes us to the very heart of this issue. The cultural landscape of the first-century Roman world awaits us.

CHAPTER 5

The Disputed Pauline Passages: Interpretation and the Search for Transcultural Principles

Come now, let us reason together.

—Isaiah 1:18a (ESV)

My husband is currently in the process of earning a seminary degree. As a result, our bookshelves have begun to overflow with theological tomes, including two rather large volumes on the topic of "hermeneutics." One of these texts (authored by a complementarian) explains this concept in the following terms:

> The great distances of time and culture between those ancient writers [of the Bible] and us require some bridges if we are to gain understanding. ... Hermeneutics provides the means for understanding the Scriptures and for applying that meaning responsibly. To avoid interpretation that is arbitrary, erroneous, or that simply suits

personal whim, the reader needs methods and principles for guidance.... Interpretation is not *either* an art *or* a science; it is *both* an art *and* a science.... We assume that people communicate in order to be understood, and this includes the authors of the Scriptures.[1]

As this makes clear, before we dive into the major passages at the center of the complementarian-egalitarian debate, we first need to understand the manner in which each side generally approaches the text of Scripture before ever cracking the cover, firing up the computer, unrolling the parchment, or whatever the case may be. This, more than anything, is what fuels the debate and yields such widely varying conclusions. In other words, it's not the text itself, but the way in which a particular side *handles and interprets* the text—and all of the assumptions that come with such a process—that separates complementarians and egalitarians, even when the text itself seems to have a rather straightforward reading.

Sarah Sumner provides two helpful examples of this in her more centrist book *Men and Women in the Church*. Consider the following passage from 1 Timothy 2:15: "But women will be saved through childbearing." A straightforward reading of this passage is absurd. Neither complementarians nor egalitarians believe that women's souls are saved through motherhood; childless women are not going to hell by virtue of dying without children. Now consider another passage from 1 Timothy 2:12: "I do not permit a woman to teach or to assume authority over a man; she must be quiet." As Sumner explains:

> There's no way to interpret this verse at face value unless we're ready to say that it is sinful for a man to learn about God from a woman. Of course most of us hold a more modified view. But that is the point. We hold a

view that differs from a straightforward reading. We say, for example, this verse restricts women from teaching the Bible "with authority" to men "publicly at the main church service in a pulpit on Sunday morning." In other words, we add extra phrases to the biblical text in order to make sense of the verse.[2]

This is where the assumptions of complementarians and egalitarians come into play—they can limit or inform the "extra phrases" that are added to make sense of the text. This lesson will be important to keep in mind as we proceed.

How to Approach the Text

I focused my studies on English literature and history when I was an undergraduate. As a student of literature, I learned that when analyzing a text it's critically important to understand the intended audience and the setting or context in which the author wrote. Notwithstanding the contrary (and confused) views of postmodernists, audience and context can never be abandoned in studying the meaning of a text; knowing *to whom* a document was written and *why* it was written cannot be separated from the ordinary meaning and use of language. You would write a letter very differently to your closest friend or spouse than you would to the cable company or the pope. As conservative complementarian Thomas Schreiner writes, "The basic rule of Bible study applies here, which says that each text must be interpreted in context."[3]

Both sides of the debate would readily agree with this principle of interpretation, regardless of their separate denominational handshakes. For example, complementarians Douglas Moo and Don Carson explain that the Gospel authors "were individuals writing in specific circumstances and to specific audiences; this historical setting, not the individual reader, must set the context for interpretation."[4] The same would certainly hold true for all of Paul's letters as well. Paul wrote to particular communities (e.g., Corinth) or ministry partners (e.g., Timothy) with whom he often (but not always, such as with the Romans) had a close personal relationship. No amount of study can provide us with the exact, divinely inspired thoughts that Paul had as he penned the words in the second chapter of his first letter to Timothy. However, we *can* use Scripture to interpret Scripture.[5] Moreover, given the relative distance in time and culture between the New Testament authors and twenty-first century readers, a commentary that provides information explaining cultural nuances can be invaluable. Just as most of us would begin with a knowledge deficit upon cracking open Homer's *Iliad*, the same can be true of many passages in the New Testament.

Because the specificity with which Paul (and other biblical authors) wrote is important for understanding meaning, it would also benefit us to keep in mind the following point emphasized by egalitarian and seminary professor Craig Keener: "My dictum for my hermeneutics students is: All Scripture is for all time, but not every Scripture is for all circumstances. When you preach from a text, make sure you get the analogy right."[6] In other words, context counts. While Paul mentions to Timothy that "all Scripture is God-breathed and is useful for teaching, rebuking, correcting and training in righteousness" (2 Tim. 3:16), it doesn't follow that Paul's intention was for us to leave common sense behind in the study and application of God's Word. Conservative complementarians like Schreiner would agree: "We must distinguish between the fundamental principle that underlies a text and the application of that principle in a specific culture."[7] Here Schreiner and Keener agree that while a biblical principle may be true for all time, the principle may not be applicable in all contexts or circumstances. For example, although Elisha summoned a bear to smite the youths who ridiculed his follicle-challenged, bald head (2 Kings 2:23–34), this is not likely a general precedent for how to respond to bullying from large crowds. Praying would certainly be a universally good option, and so too might running. All Scripture is God-breathed, but not all Scripture is applicable in each and every circumstance. Rather, good hermeneutics reminds us that we need to look to culture and context in order to determine whether a biblical principle comes into play.

Professional Hermeneutics?

How are you at diagramming Greek sentences? That is, how are you at breaking down one of Paul's arguments into individual components so that you can carefully analyze its structure? Not so great? Well, neither am I. Completing an expert Sudoku puzzle seems easier by comparison. However, I suspect that I'm not alone in this. Come to think of it, it seems highly unlikely that *any* of the recipients of Paul's letters—in the Corinthian church, the Ephesian church, or elsewhere—would have possessed such an academic-level skill honed only in seminaries. In reality, when the leaders of a church received one of Paul's letters, they most likely would have read the letter in the same manner that you or I would ordinarily read any communication that we received from a teacher, pastor, or church—without engaging in sophisticated scholarly analysis.

Why do I mention diagramming? Because of the following bizarre claim from Schreiner: "If one cannot diagram a Pauline text, then one will have difficulty in tracing the argument of that text. The ability to diagram the text and the ability to follow an argument go hand in hand."[8] Now, I have no doubt that this godly, eminent seminary professor intends well and is vastly more educated than I am. Nevertheless, this claim has a ring to it that is quite familiar from my Roman Catholic past. Within Roman Catholicism, the laity (i.e., non-priests) is not regarded as qualified to fully comprehend or interpret the Scriptures. Instead, faithful Catholics must rely upon the expertise of the church's Magisterium and the apostolic authority of the Vatican to arrive at true doctrine.[9] Since I'm a simpleton who lacks the necessary background in diagramming Pauline arguments, I suppose that 1 Timothy 2 must ultimately be above my comprehension. But before I consider conceding the debate to Schreiner based upon his diagramming prowess, I suppose that I should also express my reservation that yielding interpretive authority to those in positions of authority "because the matter is too complicated" is an approach that Protestants rejected during the Reformation. Perhaps I will press on before waving the white flag, at least for a little while longer.

In summary, both sides can agree at the outset that context is important for biblical interpretation, that Scripture interprets itself, and that unclear verses should be interpreted in light of clear ones.[10] Since these are the general ground rules of hermeneutics with which both sides of the debate are comfortable, let's proceed to the large, often pink-colored elephant in the room: the interpretation of specific Bible passages driving the debate.

Theologians in both the complementarian and egalitarian camps most vigorously debate the following passages: Genesis 1—3; 1 Corinthians 11:2–16; 1 Corinthians 14:34–35; Galatians 3:26–29; and 1 Timothy 2:9–15. This list of disputed Scripture passages is not exhaustive, but these are the primary contested passages on this issue. Since my purpose is only to provide a summary of the debate regarding the meaning and application of these verses, for the sake of brevity I will only address passages that are of greatest relevance and the most fiercely contested.

Disputed Passage #1: Galatians 3:26-29

Stephen Covey, the author of *The 7 Habits of Highly Effective People*, famously encouraged his readers to "begin with the end in mind." (I'm pretty certain this approach to biblical interpretation isn't exactly what Covey had in mind in this second habit.) For many in this debate, the *conclusion* determines the scriptural starting point. For complementarians, the starting point is 1 Timothy 2:9-15, and for egalitarians, the starting point is Galatians 3:26-29. We will look at 1 Timothy 2 later in this chapter. For now, let's look at how the Galatians passage affects our interpretative lens.

Just as Paul sent his first letter to Timothy for a particular theological purpose (largely to combat false teachings), he sent a letter to the Galatians for a similar reason. In the instance of the Galatians letter, Paul needed to clarify and defend the gospel against those who were insisting that Christians must obey the Mosaic laws of the Old Testament in order to be righteous before God. These so-called Judaizers didn't accept that it's by grace alone and through faith in Jesus Christ alone that we're justified before God (Gal. 2:15-16).[11]

Paul's comment about there being "neither Jew nor Gentile, neither slave nor free, nor is there male and female, for you are all one in Christ Jesus" (Gal. 3:28) was radical. It was so radical because the ancient world that the Galatians inhabited was more conscious of a person's social class than any Charles Dickens character or Downton Abbey dinner guest. To say that all people are redeemed through Christ—regardless of their citizenship, ethnicity, or gender—is indeed beautiful and filled with tremendous hope. However, because this verse is located within a section of Galatians that discusses our adoption as children into the promise of Abraham and the family of God, it doesn't seem to directly stand as a counterpoint to the verses in Paul's other letters that complementarians utilize to place limitations on the activities of women. The entire book of Galatians is invaluable for comprehending the gospel and the way that it's lived out between men and women (Galatians 2:20 is my favorite verse!), but it isn't necessarily the "checkmate" to conservative complementarians' arguments that egalitarians might seek. Indeed, given its context and the power structures that it addresses, Galatians 3:26–29 likely has little to do with the role of women in ministry, being much more relevant within other cultural contexts such as marriage. As egalitarian Gordon Fee notes:

> Cultural structures simply exist.... In Paul's view, one can serve Christ well within such limits. What he disallows is giving *significance* to structures and roles as such. Because when one does this, the Jew will demand that the Gentile be circumcised, the husband will want his wife to be his servant, and Philemon can take Onesimus back only as a slave, not as a brother.[12]

While both genders are redeemed and one in Christ, our differences do still exist, and we need to build one another up to live in a manner worthy of the high price that was paid to redeem us (1 Cor. 6:20).[13]

Disputed Passage #2: Genesis 1—3

Let me say a few words about Genesis 1—3. Many complementarians confidently assert that this unbroken theme of universal male headship in the local church is taught in Genesis, but this is far from certain. Grounding the argument in a "theme" from the narrative of Genesis 1—3 can be particularly difficult because of the Hebrew source language and the text's basic narrative format. For example, complementarians make much of the way that men and women were created, assigned tasks, rebuked for sin, and received different types of punishment for their sin. The specific use of ᶜēzer, or the Hebrew word translated as "helper," is a prominent theme for both sides. But at the end of the creation narrative, we still fundamentally have a first husband and a first wife—a first marriage—not a first pastor and a first female congregant. Since it seems valid to separate the verses that pertain to marriage, including the relationship between spouses, from the more general passages regarding women in the church, I will limit the exegetical discussion to 1 Corinthians 11 and 1 Timothy 2, which are the most disputed passages of all.[14]

Disputed Passage #3: 1 Corinthians 11:3-16

Let's start with 1 Corinthians 11:3-16. It's important to read the entire passage in context, so here it is in full:

> [3] But I want you to realize that the head of every man is Christ, and the head of the woman is man, and the head of Christ is God. [4] Every man who prays or prophesies with his head covered dishonors his head. [5] But every woman who prays or prophesies with her head uncovered dishonors her head—it is the same as having her head shaved. [6] For if a woman does not cover her head, she might as well have her hair cut off; but if it is a disgrace for a woman to have her hair cut off or her head shaved, then she should cover her head. [7] A man ought not to cover his head, since he is the image and glory of God; but

woman is the glory of man. ⁸ For man did not come from woman, but woman from man; ⁹ neither was man created for woman, but woman for man. ¹⁰ It is for this reason that a woman ought to have authority over her own head, because of the angels. ¹¹ Nevertheless, in the Lord woman is not independent of man, nor is man independent of woman. ¹² For as woman came from man, so also man is born of woman. But everything comes from God. ¹³ Judge for yourselves: Is it proper for a woman to pray to God with her head uncovered? ¹⁴ Does not the very nature of things teach you that if a man has long hair, it is a disgrace to him, ¹⁵ but that if a woman has long hair, it is her glory? For long hair is given to her as a covering. ¹⁶ If anyone wants to be contentious about this, we have no other practice—nor do the churches of God.

As a young Christian, I distinctly recall reading this passage and being initially troubled by it at a deep level. Although I attended private Roman Catholic schools for more than twelve years, never had I encountered this passage in any of my Scripture classes, and consequently I was quite startled to read it.

This passage is a good example of how a portion of Scripture can contain both clear and unclear language. There is still much that is unclear about what woman being the "glory of man" or "because of the angels" entails. Different scholars emphasize different elements of the passage in support of their own positions; however, the most interesting element in the overarching discussion, at least for our present purposes, is the mention of both head coverings (likely a veil) and human creation *in the same passage*. It's true that the context seems to suggest that this is a passage primarily about marriage, although the metaphor used is complex and mysterious. But even complementarians who reference this passage as "clear" evidence in support of male headship within marriage don't know why the angels are involved or how to carefully square this passage with the Genesis account of both men and women being made in the image of God.[15] If you press the language too literally, you run the risk of quickly undermining the *Imago Dei*, or image of God, that all women bear (Gen. 1:27) and requiring a universal cultural standard of female head covering.[16]

If the plain reading of Scripture is usually the preferable one, then by all means let's drive to the nearest haberdashery to purchase veils, because women shouldn't enter a public assembly to worship without their heads covered. Though many complementarian churches staunchly prevent women from teaching men in most or all capacities (in order to be faithful to 1 Timothy 2), they don't seem to turn away women who have inadvertently left their hats or veils at home. I, for one, would like to see some consistency on this matter, and it has nothing to do with my English love for hats (or the fact that a veil would cover up the sad truth that I have not been introduced yet to a hairdryer or hair products).[17] As we'll see shortly when we take a much closer look at 1 Timothy 2:9–15, the created order is referenced by Paul in *each* of these passages, with respect to both women's head coverings *and* the possibility of women teaching or having authority over men. It's therefore strange that only the latter and not the former should be applied to Christian women in our time.[18] Why do we see such unequal application? As Keener comments, "We cannot consistently require a transcultural application prohibiting women's teaching or holding authority based on 1 Timothy 2:11–12 without also requiring all married women to cover their heads in keeping with 1 Corinthians 11:2–16 (a point Paul, in fact, argues at much greater length)."[19]

Complementarians are not unaware of this charge of inconsistency, and Schreiner has attempted to answer it:

> [I]t is *rhetorically effective* for egalitarians to say that women must wear head coverings today. But such a comment is *hermeneutically unpersuasive*, for the complementarian argument from texts like 1 Tim. 2:11–15 is deeper than egalitarians apparently perceive. We are not saying that we must invariably reproduce the customs of the biblical text in our culture. We are arguing that there are *contextual indicators* (the order of creation in 1 Cor. 11:8–9 and 1 Tim. 2:13) that the regulations and prohibitions in these passages are transcultural.[20]

In other words, highlighting that the creation narrative is used in both passages may *sound* persuasive at first, but to Schreiner it isn't all that convincing.[21]

In Schreiner's opinion, it's *merely* "rhetorically effective"—it only sounds impressive—to link Paul's head covering passage (1 Cor. 11:3-16) with the complementarians' chief passage (1 Tim. 2:9-15), and thereby insist that *both* of Paul's instructions be treated as transcultural principles. However, despite Schreiner's protests to the contrary, I see this as "hermeneutically persuasive" as well. To understand why, note once more what Schreiner writes: "We are arguing that there are *contextual indicators* [such as the order of creation] that the regulations and prohibitions in these passages are transcultural." In the same article, Schreiner also makes the following comment: "It should be said ... that an argument from the [Old Testament] based on the created order is almost certainly transcultural."[22] Schreiner is therefore quite clear that Paul's reference to the created order necessarily implies that we should be on the lookout for a transcultural principle in *both* passages. And yet, despite the straightforward reading of 1 Corinthians 11:3–16, Schreiner (and many others like him) concludes that the transcultural principle is *not* that women should universally wear head coverings: "Also, while wearing head coverings no longer speaks to our culture, there is an abiding principle in this text that is applicable to the twentieth century."[23] Importantly, in this instance Schreiner concludes that Paul's reference to the created order is *insufficient* to overrule the cultural context of the passage for purposes of modern interpretation and application. With respect to 1 Corinthians 11:3–16, cultural considerations relevant to the passage overcome any plain reading that may be suggested by the mention of the created order, and as a result women need no longer wear head coverings.

However, Schreiner takes the *opposite* approach with respect to 1 Timothy 2:9–15. As we'll soon see, this highly debated passage also invokes the created order, but here complementarians like Schreiner conclude that it's now *sufficient* to overrule the cultural context of the passage when discerning "an abiding principle in th[e] text that is applicable to the twentieth century." As a result, it's still the case that women shouldn't be permitted to teach or have authority over men. In short, we have one instance where a plain reading combined with an argument from creation (i.e., head coverings) is accepted as culturally *relative* by a significant majority of theologians,[24] and another instance *by the same author* where a plain reading combined with an argument from creation (i.e., teaching and authority) is deemed to necessarily override the cultural and other contextual factors that suggest a culturally relative requirement that is no longer applicable. It's difficult not to notice this unequal treatment, and dismissing the criticism as a "rhetorically effective" ploy does nothing to answer the charge of inconsistency.[25] Furthermore, it's difficult not to notice that, at least according to Schreiner, Paul's use of the created order overrides context and culture in a way that perfectly aligns with Schreiner's own broader theological perspective on gender roles.

To egalitarians, this is a clear example of a fallacy known as "special pleading," or an argument in which the advocate deliberately ignores aspects that are unfavorable to his or her point of view. From a practical standpoint, it makes no sense to insist that women wear head coverings to church in the twenty-first century, even though Paul tied them to the created order. Common sense suggests that Paul had a cultural reason for including this requirement in his letter (e.g., to protect female slaves from sexual assault),[26] and since we now live in a very different context, the specific requirement (wear head coverings) no longer applies even though the underlying principle (female protection) is, as Schreiner argues, transcultural. To repeat Keener's dictum, "All Scripture is for all time, but not every Scripture is for all circumstances."

However, why can't the same be true of other passages, such as 1 Timothy 2:9–15, that *also* mention the created order? As we'll soon see, this is precisely what egalitarians strenuously argue. To borrow Schreiner's words, the transcultural "regulations and prohibitions" suggested by the "contextual indicators" have nothing to do with some sort of God-ordained male-female order, but rather Paul's common-sense rule—that is still enormously relevant today—against permitting uneducated individuals to lead a church. More on that in a moment.

The important point is that both egalitarians and complementarians look for transcultural principles when the created order is invoked, but Schreiner insists that egalitarians are wrong because "the complementarian argument... is deeper than egalitarians apparently perceive."[27] I'm not sure what this mysterious reference to "deeper" means, but Keener has an apt challenge for those who argue as Schreiner does: "Must a transcultural application be absurd before we will limit it? Or do these 'absurd' examples point out the way we consistently ought to read Paul's letters? To claim that only the *obviously* culturally limited passages are in fact culturally limited is simply to beg the question of interpretation methods."[28] In fact, Keener cites several other examples where Paul gives very specific or culturally relative instructions (e.g., holy kisses) that would never be pressed in the same manner as the verses that mention women and wives. So while Schreiner sifts out a principle from the text of 1 Corinthians 11:3–16, rather than an absurd application that would universally require women to wear head coverings, the same approach seems to be arbitrarily denied to egalitarians when considering 1 Timothy 2:9–15. Complementarians like Schreiner dismiss the creation connection between these passages only by means of special pleading and vague explanations.

Disputed Passage #4: 1 Timothy 2:9–15

We're now in a position to consider the central passage in this debate. Once more, what Paul wrote is worth reading in full:

> [9] I also want the women to dress modestly, with decency and propriety, adorning themselves, not with elaborate hairstyles or gold or pearls or expensive clothes, [10] but with good deeds, appropriate for women who profess to worship God. [11] A woman should learn in quietness and

full submission. ¹²I do not permit a woman to teach or to assume authority over a man; she must be quiet. ¹³For Adam was formed first, then Eve. ¹⁴And Adam was not the one deceived; it was the woman who was deceived and became a sinner. ¹⁵But women will be saved through childbearing—if they continue in faith, love and holiness with propriety.

Paul's first epistle to Timothy, and these seven verses in particular, have prompted so much intense discussion and generated so many volumes of scholarship that it can feel daunting to even begin examining this passage. I mentioned in chapter 1 that Schreiner and Köstenberger have written a book in excess of 300 pages just on these seven verses, setting forth their conclusions regarding women in ministry.[29] Not unreasonably, some might conclude from the depth of the academic study devoted to this issue that these verses are anything but "clear" or amenable to a "plain reading." Indeed, the amount of scholarship committed to this sliver of Paul's total work should prompt hesitation before any firm doctrines on gender theology are carved into stone. With Paul's talk of women remaining "quiet" and being "saved through childbearing," I suppose a fair amount of spirited debate was inevitable.

By my estimation, the debate between conservative complementarians and egalitarians over 1 Timothy 2:9–15 fundamentally boils down to four issues: (1) the education of women in Greco-Roman society during the first century; (2) the meaning of an obscure Greek word that is used only once in the entire New Testament; (3) Paul's use of the creation account in this passage; and (4) the connection between salvation, child birth, and worship of the Greek goddess

Artemis. Each of these four points of dispute will be considered in turn.

Issue #1: The Education of Women in First-Century Greco-Roman Society

Many scholars note that in relation to previous generations and cultures, women in Ephesus were not the isolated, illiterate, social recluses that they once had been. There certainly is evidence for this based on the records of women participating in society in new ways.[30] New Testament scholar S. M. Baugh, a contributor to the book co-authored by Schreiner and Köstenberger, observes that "Upper-class women participated in other forms of education in Ephesus, particularly private lectures in salons.... Because women's education in antiquity usually took place privately, we only get a glimpse of it here and there in historical sources."[31] Baugh goes on to provide a catalogue of some of the inscriptions and tributes to women that are available in ancient sources in order to highlight that there were *some* educated women in Ephesus when Paul penned his letter to Timothy.

While this initially may seem to fly in the face of the notion that women were lacking in formal education during this period of antiquity, it bears mentioning that Baugh's data pertains to "upper class women." A slight uptick in the educational status of women or, more specifically, the status of very wealthy women, hardly seems to translate to a well-educated and independent female population. We have no historical reason to think that middle or lower class women—or poor women or female slaves—were similarly educated. The vast majority of women were, for all intents and purposes, still very much the possession of their "paterfamilias," meaning the male head of a family or household. The most telling evidence of women's value—or rather their lack thereof—in the general society can be seen through the population crisis at that time:

> The low value of the female in the society was also reflected in the widespread practices of infanticide and abandonment of female babies. It was very common to raise only one daughter per family, which, together with maternal mortality, contributed to a shortage of women during the Roman Empire that created a population crisis.[32]

If a society can be judged in part by what it does with the most fragile members within its ranks, then the Romans as a whole were no champions of women's rights or human rights in general. A Roman letter penned around 1 B.C. is illustrative: "If—good luck to you!—you bear offspring, if it is a male, let it live; if it is a female, expose it."[33] If a family desired only one daughter, and left additional daughters to die from abandonment and exposure, there is very little historical reason to think that women without significant financial means would have been deemed worthy of an educational investment that could have gone to a son instead.

This point is significant for understanding the cultural context of Paul's letter to Timothy. Specifically, because women in Ephesus were for the most part highly *uneducated*, this meant that they would have been expected, as a matter of custom and culture, to learn quietly without disturbing the progress of the group's study by asking basic or fundamental questions. Keener explains why:

> I had always found most plausible the view that women were interrupting the [church] service with questions. But I never could imagine what circumstances provoked

these public questions until I read Plutarch's essay *On Lectures*. Then I realized that listeners regularly interrupted lectures with questions, whether to learn more about the subject or to compete intellectually with an inadequately prepared lecturer. I quickly realized that questions were common in Jewish settings as well and were a regular part of ancient Mediterranean lecture settings in general.[34]

This precedent is similarly found in some of the Pauline verses about women remaining silent in the church and asking their husbands questions at home rather than in the assembly (1 Cor. 14:34–35). While this may sound sexist to our modern ears, Keener argues that Paul wrote such an instruction to promote good order:

> [I]f we read Paul less anachronistically, in his own social context it would have helped the women as well as establishing order. Paul implicitly makes husbands responsible for their wives' tutoring. . . . Paul avoids social impropriety by advising the women to avoid questioning other men during the Christian education component of the gathering, but he is not against their learning. Yet . . . their lack of learning may have been precisely part of the problem. With greater understanding, they might become better able to articulate themselves intellectually in the same assemblies in which they could pray and prophesy. *Viewed in this light, the real issues are not gender but propriety and learning—neither of which need restrain women's voices in the church today.*[35]

It's true that some women, such as Paul's ministry partner Priscilla (Acts 18:18; Rom. 16:3; 2 Tim. 4:19), may have moved well beyond the theological basics.[36] However, from the historical context it's likely that a majority of Christian women in Ephesus were uneducated and left to grapple (with the help of their husbands) with the fundamentals of the faith. If such women had brought their multitude of questions to an assembled worship service, the entire body of believers would have experienced a slower growth rate as well.

In some law schools today (such as the one my husband attended), the professors will allow unprepared students—meaning those who have not read the assigned cases for the day—to sit in a separate part of the lecture hall and thereby acknowledge their lack of preparation. This is permitted several times per semester, and it's actually encouraged because a student's lack of preparation could disrupt the progress of the class and waste valuable time. Professors would rather grant the occasional allowance to their students rather than risk a delay, and as a result everyone benefits. From what we've already seen, ancient writers like Plutarch and Paul would likely have applauded this idea. The law school approach closely parallels the approach Paul articulates in his letters, helping us to recapture some of the specific cultural nuances that may be lost on the modern reader.

So on the whole, while we do have examples of first-century women enjoying new roles in the city of Ephesus, their access to education would almost certainly have been more limited than a man's access and almost entirely determined by their socio-economic status. As Keener observes, "If the problem with the Ephesian women was their lack of education and consequent susceptibility to false teaching, the text provides us a concrete local example of a more general principle: *Those most susceptible to false teaching should not teach.*"[37] This last sentence is one of the key points of contention between complementarians and egalitarians. Where complementarians see unchanging gender roles in Paul's writings, egalitarians see prohibitions and requirements imposed by the cultural context, specifically the lack of female education in ancient society. Regardless of your position on this issue, it does seem to make a great deal of sense to prohibit uneducated Christians from serving as teachers or holding positions of authority. After all, how can someone teach what she doesn't know or combat false doctrines if she doesn't know true theology? For egalitarians, this is the transcultural principle inherent in 1 Timothy 2:9–15, and it applied to women in Ephesus because they were largely uneducated. Now that women are generally quite educated in many cases, the prohibition is no longer needed, unless it's based upon God's design as complementarians contend.

Issue #2: The Meaning of an Obscure Greek Word

In his letter, Paul writes that he does "not permit a woman to teach or to assume authority over a man; she must be quiet" (1 Tim. 2:12). The Greek word for "authority" is *authenteō*, and its meaning is another murky topic because it appears only once in all of the New Testament. In the standard Greek of Paul's day, the usual word for "authority" that Paul could have selected was *exousia*, which is used over a hundred times in the New Testament.[38] However, Paul clearly thought a different word—a less common word—was needed in this particular circumstance. The question is why Paul thought so.

When biblical scholars wish to understand a rare word, they sometimes look to other writings in the hopes of finding new insights. For example, an Old Testament scholar might look to Ugaritic, an extinct Semitic language, to better understand a Hebrew term. Likewise, New Testament scholars can look to extra-biblical Greek writings, such as plays, biographies, and speeches, to better understand how a word was used in a broader non-Christian context. Unfortunately, the extra-biblical examples of *authenteō* are also sparse, which further complicates matters. The meanings of *authenteō* outside of the New Testament span from "murder" to "rule over."

This sparse textual evidence has not prevented New Testament scholars from trying to tease out the best definition of *authenteō*, although the results are anything but consistent. For example, complementarian Al Wolters conducted an in-depth study of the verb as it's used throughout *all* known Greek writings, concluding that its meaning is quite close to the usual term of authority (i.e., *exousia*) and lacks any sort of negative undertone (such as "murder").[39] Egalitarian Linda Belleville conducted a similar study, but based on the same evidence she concluded that the meaning of the verb is closer to "domineer" or "have your way with," both of which are negative.[40] No one on either side of this debate would object to a transcultural principle against "domineering," as such conduct would be inconsistent with the loving example of Christ.

Furthermore, Köstenberger argues that these two verbs, "to teach" and "to have authority," fit a pattern of paired infinitives that can be seen elsewhere in the New Testament and in extra-biblical literature as well. According to Köstenberger, when two Greek words are paired together in this manner they must both be lexically similar, meaning both must be positive or negative in their use. Because Paul uses the regular term for "teach" (*didaskō*), rather than a more negative term such as "false teacher" (*pseudodidaskalos*), Köstenberger concludes that the meaning of *authenteō* must also be generally positive (rather than negative or neutral) due to the Greek syntax of the sentence.[41]

Further examples abound, but the point seems clear.

Whether or not the meaning of *authenteō* is negative is what matters. If the meaning is negative, then the egalitarian argument is supported because Paul is prohibiting women from behaving in a very unkind manner, which is far different from prohibiting women from having "authority." Oppositely, if the meaning is positive, the complementarian argument is supported. However, this point of contention will likely never be settled. Because the textual evidence is somewhat ambiguous, as demonstrated by the different conclusions reached by credentialed New Testament scholars who have examined *all* of the available data, it doesn't seem unreasonable to infer not only that the "feeling" of *authenteō* is uncertain but also that its meaning is, at a minimum, not *precisely* synonymous for "authority."

Issue #3: Paul's Use of the Creation Account

Even if the Greek terms for "teach" and "authority" are both positive, as complementarians like Köstenberger claim, this alone doesn't settle the matter. At this point, the debate shifts to the manner in which Paul went about explaining his reasons for this prohibition. The search for "transcultural" or lasting norms is important because the most conservative complementarians use 1 Timothy 2:12–14 as a sort of "creation defense" for imposing strict limitations on the use of women's spiritual gifts within the local church.

At the outset, it's important to note additional cultural factors that inform the context. We have already seen that in Ephesus most women were uneducated, unless they happened to be very wealthy. Further compounding the problem for ancient women is that they were also regarded as *untrustworthy*. Walter Liefeld, who self-identifies as a "pluralist" rather than an egalitarian,[42] offers the following analysis of what "teaching" meant at the time of Paul's letter:

> The "teaching" prohibited to women in 1 Timothy was not the explanation of biblical texts, since the Bible was not yet complete or widely disseminated. At that time teaching meant the transmission of the apostolic tradition. The authoritative teachings of the Lord Jesus and of the apostles were transmitted at first in an oral form before they were universally available in written form in the New Testament. But it must be recognized that the witness to such a tradition would not have been accepted from the mouths of women, who were considered unreliable as witnesses. Whatever the theological or circumstantial reasons Paul had for prohibiting women from teaching, the fact is that this teaching depended on the authority of the teacher in a way that it does not today.[43]

In other words, there was no NIV Study Bible that could be consulted to evaluate the truth of the teacher's message. Only the verbal gospel message was present in most settings, and many audiences would never trust a female messenger. (Phoebe delivered the letter from Paul to the Romans, but she didn't need to covey any verbal teaching of her own in this instance, just the physical letter.) Furthermore, women (especially widows) were vulnerable to false teachers because of their lack of training. Keener explains why:

> [I]t can hardly be coincidence that the one passage that is most restrictive (1 Tim. 2:11–12) also appears in the one set of letters in the Bible that we specifically know addressed a congregation where false teachers were

targeting women. This claim is explicit in 2 Timothy 3:6–7, and is probable in 1 Timothy 5:13, where some widows are spreading a form of "nonsense." Since false teachers needed homes for house churches, it made most sense to target the most theologically vulnerable homeowners: widows who owned homes on account of widowhood and had less access to training because of their gender.[44]

Therefore, Christian women in Ephesus were regarded as untrustworthy, largely uneducated, and consequently susceptible to the unholy plans of false teachers. If this is the historical context in which Paul's letter is set—and the evidence seems to suggest as much—then Paul had a valid reason for denying women the opportunity to teach or exercise authority. Arguably, they would have been quite unsuited to the task. But in our modern American setting, with Title IX in place since 1972 and publicly funded education available to girls and women, would Paul have penned these same words?

Recall Schreiner's claim: "[Complementarians] are not saying that we must invariably reproduce the customs of the biblical text in our culture. We are arguing that there are *contextual indicators* (the order of creation in 1 Cor. 11:8–9 and 1 Tim. 2:13) that the regulations and prohibitions in these passages are transcultural."[45] According to Schreiner and other conservative complementarians, Paul *would* have penned these same words even in the twenty-first century, as suggested by Paul's "contextual indicator" of the created order. However, egalitarians object to focusing solely (or primarily) on this *single* contextual indicator (i.e., the created order) to the exclusion of all *other* contextual indicators in 1 Timothy 2:9–15.

As egalitarians might ask, what about the contextual indicators in 1 Timothy indicating that false teaching was a problem in the Ephesian church? For example, Paul instructed

Timothy to "stay there in Ephesus so that [he] may command certain people not to teach false doctrines any longer" (1 Tim. 1:3). Since the women in Ephesus were uneducated and therefore susceptible to these false teachers (2 Tim. 3:6–7), why shouldn't 1 Timothy 2:12 ("I do not permit a woman to teach or to assume authority over a man") be understood as setting forth a transcultural principle that prohibits unqualified and uneducated individuals from serving as teachers? Stated differently, why does the created order override all other contextual indicators, including one as obvious as the condition of Ephesian women? Why the apparent inconsistency?

Against Schreiner's objection, this is not a "rhetorically effective" ploy but an essential question, one that strikes at the heart of what egalitarians perceive as a self-serving double standard. Indeed, egalitarians are taking Schreiner seriously when he insists that "[v]irtually all scholars agree that the circumstances addressed in New Testament documents affect the theme emphasized by the writers."[46] In light of the circumstances in Ephesus, why couldn't Paul's theme have been to prohibit unqualified individuals (in this case women) from holding leadership positions, rather than laying down timeless gender roles for the church? When an exegetical approach is inconsistently applied, it can signal a deeper worldview commitment that effectively steers the biblical interpretation to a conclusion that is consistent with the interpreter's assumptions. Such inconsistencies highlight the weakness in the brickwork of a person's argument. Both sides of the debate seem to have done this from time to time, but it can be telling *when* this is done and with what goal in mind.[47]

Not surprisingly, complementarians haven't taken such accusations lying down. Some scholars argue that Paul's introduction of the creation narrative serves to provide a blueprint for his prohibition to become transcultural, meaning

Women's Gifts, Women's Roles 73

its application is divorced from any cultural influences at the time of authorship. As Schreiner points out when he engages with Keener:

> Craig [Keener] also argues that not all proof texts from the [Old Testament] are transcultural, and that the [Old Testament] could be used analogously, without any notion of a transcultural application. Craig raises an important and complex issue that deserves more discussion than is possible here. It should be said in reply that an argument from the [Old Testament] based on the created order is almost certainly transcultural. Jesus argued from creation in defending monogamy and God's intention that husbands and wives should not divorce (Matt. 19:3–9); Paul argued from creation in prohibiting homosexuality (Rom. 1:26–27). There is no reason, in the case of 1 Timothy 2:13, to think Paul is only arguing analogically. Paul prohibits women from teaching and exercising authority over men because of God's intention in creating men and women.[48]

Schreiner is certainly correct that Jesus and Paul defended transcultural moral principles using the created order. But here Schreiner's previous comment that "the circumstances addressed in New Testament documents affect the theme emphasized by the writers" becomes quite relevant. We have already seen that a reference to creation or Adam and Eve in one of Paul's letters is not always a signal that the *plain reading* of the text is transcultural. Once again, recall Keener's observations regarding Paul's requirement for head coverings in connection with the created order in 1 Corinthians 11:3–16. Most complementarians would not insist on a literal application of this passage in our modern churches, even though they do so in the case of 1 Timothy 2:9–15. In summary, the situation looks something like this:

> 1 Corinthians 11:3–16 → creation + cultural factors → plain reading is *not* transcultural
>
> 1 Timothy 2:9–15 → creation + cultural factors → plain reading *is* transcultural

Both sides of the debate agree that a transcultural principle is present in each passage. For conservative complementarians like Schreiner, this differing outcome is to be expected because "the complementarian argument from texts like 1 Tim. 2:11–15 is deeper than egalitarians apparently perceive."[49] However, what complementarians see as "deeper" is to egalitarians just special pleading by another name.

And so we're at an impasse, with no clear resolution in sight. So let's ask a different question instead. If complementarians like Grudem, Piper, and Schreiner are correct, what is the logical outworking of their position? It would seem to be that God either intended to create women with fewer gifts or, alternatively, with fewer options to develop and use the gifts that they have. There are no other possibilities. If Paul's transcultural principle is that women should always be prohibited from teaching or having authority over men in the local church, then either the Spirit doesn't grant women the gift of teaching (see 1 Cor. 12:4–11), thereby saving church elders a great deal of time by shrinking the pool of aspiring female teachers close to zero, or else the Spirit does grant women the gift of teaching, but God's plan for the church limits women in the exercise and development of this gift. As Schreiner writes, female prophets "transmit the word of the Lord; they do not study, prepare, and then deliver the word of the Lord."[50] The implication from this comment is clear: women are permitted to be *prophets* but prohibited from *preaching*. But since they cannot preach, they may also have less incentive to study the Bible at an in-depth level or be given less theological training, whether intentionally or not. J. D. Greear, the new president of the Southern Baptist Convention, has forthrightly admitted as much:

> Sometimes, in our rightful espousal of complementarianism, we in the SBC have failed to create the same pathways into ministry for women that we have for men. This was true at the church that I pastor: it was easy for men to get trained and step into leadership, but not women. Our ministry team was very, very male-heavy, as we tended to consider only men even for positions of leadership that really did not require occupation by an ordained pastor/elder.[51]

Sadly, I witnessed some of this firsthand, although in a more subtle form, during my years at a complementarian local church.[52]

Many in the twenty-first century would have their hackles up after reading the conclusions of conservative complementarians, and I will address that in later chapters when we examine gifting and roles. However, other implications naturally follow from the conservative complementarian position. Indeed, if the creation narrative undergirds and serves as the basis for the primary male-female structure within modern churches, we have to ask whether we aren't wrongly failing to apply *other* relevant applications from the opening chapters of Genesis. Might we need to make some other drastic changes within the local church? Given the employment options available to Adam and Eve, should godly people be limited merely to farming and zoological pursuits? Is taxonomy—the branch of science concerned with naming and classification—one of the highest vocations to which one can aspire? Should all modern technological advancements be thrown out, including smart phones, indoor plumbing, video game consoles, and curling irons?

Obviously, these suggestions are ridiculous, and intentionally so. The opening chapters of Genesis *describe* the conditions in which Adam and Eve lived and how things came to be. In doing so, the creation narrative doesn't regulate the living conditions for later human beings in such a way as to proscribe future employment roles or technologies of which Adam and Eve had no knowledge. However, since Adam and Eve were the first married couple, rather than a male pastor and a female congregant, might the same also be said for gender roles? In other words, is it really a foregone conclusion that women should never teach men in any capacity, even if they are gifted teachers redeemed by the atoning work of our Savior, simply because Eve was deceived?[53]

Complementarians would respond that male-female hierarchy was established *before* sin and death entered the world through the sin of Adam and Eve,[54] and that the very creation act alone demonstrates the differing roles between men and women. Indeed, much is made of the differing ways in which God speaks to Adam and Eve regarding their sins. Even so, both sides of the debate reach very different conclusions from the same starting point in the Genesis narrative; a determinative resolution in the near future once again seems unlikely.

I'll conclude this section by noting that complementarians could be making an incorrect assumption. There could very well be an element within the mystery of marriage—including the "first" marriage of Adam and Eve—that is simply not transferable to the church community as a whole. Indeed, from passages like Ephesians 5:22–33 we see that marriage and the local church are only analogous to a certain extent. Perhaps wrongly, conservative complementarians often set aside the marriage component of the first couple and focus solely on their genders and respective sins. As this relates to 1 Timothy 2:9–15, Keener's insight seems on point:

> In this case, Paul is drawing an analogy between the easily deceived Eve and the easily deceived women in Ephesus. Since Paul elsewhere uses Eve as an analogy for the gullibility of the whole Corinthian church (2 Cor. 11:3)—the men no less than the women—it is clear that he does not simply regard Eve as a standard symbol for women, any more than the consequences of Adam's fall apply only to men in other Pauline passages (Rom. 5:12–21; 1 Cor. 15:45–49).[55]

The analogy highlighted by Keener is also of significance in responding to one of Schreiner's objections. With regard to *why* Paul wrote that he does "not permit a woman to teach or to assume authority over a man" (1 Tim. 2:12), Schreiner argues that "Paul could have easily said that women are prohibited from teaching because they were spreading the false teaching or because of their lack of education. Instead he appeals to the created order."[56] Certainly, it would help the egalitarians make their case if Paul had done so. But Paul didn't merely reference the created order: "For Adam was formed first, then Eve. And Adam was not the one deceived; it was the woman who was deceived and became a sinner" (1 Tim. 2:13–14). The reference to Eve's deception is *not* part of the created order, so why mention it at all? Some explanation must be given, and Keener's suggestion doesn't seem at all implausible in light of what we can historically infer was occurring in Ephesus.

Issue #4: The Connection Between Salvation, Child Birth, and Worship of the Greek Goddess Artemis

"But women will be saved through childbearing—if they continue in faith, love and holiness with propriety" (1 Tim. 2:15). Given the preceding verses, it doesn't seem unreasonable to say that Paul's concluding thought was a strange one, at least on a plain reading of the text. On its face, what does this have to do with female teaching and authority? And what does childbearing have to do with salvation? Has Paul haphazardly jumped from church order to salvation? Once again, cultural context is key for understanding Paul.

Have you ever chanted for two hours straight? Such zeal may certainly be expected from an impassioned crowd at the latest Taylor Swift concert. However, the Ephesian idol of Paul's day was no living, breathing musician but rather a goddess of their culture's creation: Artemis. Not only did she sustain the local economy, but she captured the hearts of the people. Luke describes this well in the following passage:

> [23] About that time there arose a great disturbance about the Way. [24] A silversmith named Demetrius, who made silver shrines of Artemis, brought in a lot of business for the craftsmen there. [25] He called them together, along with the workers in related trades, and said: "You know, my friends, that we receive a good income from this business. [26] And you see and hear how this fellow Paul has convinced and led astray large numbers of people here in Ephesus and in practically the whole province of Asia. He says that gods made by human hands are no gods at all. [27] There is danger not only that our trade will lose its good name, but also that the temple of the great goddess

Artemis will be discredited; and the goddess herself, who is worshiped throughout the province of Asia and the world, will be robbed of her divine majesty."

[28] When they heard this, they were furious and began shouting: "Great is Artemis of the Ephesians!" [29] Soon the whole city was in an uproar. The people seized Gaius and Aristarchus, Paul's traveling companions from Macedonia, and all of them rushed into the theater together. [30] Paul wanted to appear before the crowd, but the disciples would not let him. [31] Even some of the officials of the province, friends of Paul, sent him a message begging him not to venture into the theater.

[32] The assembly was in confusion: Some were shouting one thing, some another. Most of the people did not even know why they were there. [33] The Jews in the crowd pushed Alexander to the front, and they shouted instructions to him. He motioned for silence in order to make a defense before the people. [34] But when they realized he was a Jew, they all shouted in unison for about two hours: "Great is Artemis of the Ephesians!"[57]

Because Paul's letter to Timothy was sent to the city of Ephesus (1 Tim. 1:3), where Timothy was serving as a young leader in the Ephesian church, it seems like a reasonable inference that Artemis was somewhat of a hometown hero in the pagan god circuit among Timothy's potential converts. Artemis was to Ephesus what LeBron James is to Cleveland, Ohio. (You didn't think you would get any good sports analogies in here, did you?) So if this was the setting in which Timothy was serving when he received Paul's letter, it appears that Artemis—and all things pagan that she stood for—was well-steeped in the Ephesian drinking water. Linda Belleville is an egalitarian, and her reflections on this scene from Acts and 1 Timothy, both of which involve the city of Ephesus, are quite interesting:

> One explanation is that they were influenced by the cult of Artemis, where the female was exalted and considered superior to the male. The importance of this cult to the citizens of Ephesus in Paul's day is evident from Luke's record of their two-hour chant—"Great is Artemis of the Ephesians" (Acts 19:28, 34).[58]

Indeed, much depended on Artemis. Baugh explains just how important Artemis—and her temple—was to the city of Ephesus:

> Ephesus was not a temple-city like the oracular centers of Claros or Delphi, yet the worship of Artemis Ephesia dominated the city in many ways. The Artemisium [i.e., the temple of Artemis] itself was the largest building in the Greek world, about four times larger than the Athenian Parthenon. It boasted 127 massive columns decorated with friezes. Its adornments by some of the most famous painters and sculptors of antiquity made it one of the Seven Wonders of the Ancient World. Hence its fame.... The Artemisium's tourist appeal brought "no small income" to the whole city, including the silversmith guild (Acts 19:24–27).... The Artemisium illustrates the intimate connection between the economic and the religious spheres of life at Ephesus.[59]

Even for those who think that some commentators overemphasize the influence of Artemis on Ephesian society, and therefore by association on Paul's letter to Timothy, the imposing presence of the Artemisium, along with the integration of

Artemis worship into all aspects of Ephesian society, cannot be denied based on the historical data. The rioting episode that Belleville references from Acts 19 could have been heavily motivated by commercial pursuits, since the idol-making business was the Apple or Facebook of its day. Even so, those who supported this industry must have had strong emotional and religious reasons for purchasing their Artemis statues. Moreover, Artemis was especially dear to women. Not only was the Artemisium the largest building in the Greek world, with Artemis temple worship a focus of daily commercial and religious life, this particular pagan goddess was the patron deity of something critical to roughly half the Ephesian population: childbirth.

According to Blomberg, one of the general hermeneutical considerations for Paul's letters is that "interpreters must locate them as specifically as possible in a particular historical context."[60] He elaborates:

> Fortunately, at least with the Pauline Epistles, a close reading of a given letter from start to finish usually discloses specific details about the letter's audience and relevant circumstances.... Thus, we can learn much about opponents in Philippi from references in the letter itself (Phil 1:15–18; 3:2–11). We may appreciate the superstitious, pagan attitudes Paul encountered in Galatia by reading background material in Acts (cf. Acts 14:11–13 with Gal 3:1). And we can understand why Paul wrote extensively about sexual morality in 1 Corinthians (5:1–13; 6:12–20; 7:1–40) when we learn from other historical sources that the massive temple to Aphrodite, which towered over the city of Corinth from a nearby cliff-top, had at one time employed over 1,000 "sacred prostitutes"—male and female![61]

Therefore, whether you are egalitarian or complementarian, it's critical to understand what life was like for women in Ephesus. Just as Aphrodite is relevant to understanding 1 Corinthians, Artemis is relevant to understanding 1 Timothy.

At the time Paul wrote his letter to Timothy, childbearing was a leading cause of death for women in Ephesus, including childbirth itself, pregnancy, and the health implications resulting therefrom. As Baugh explains:

> [A]n estimated 50 percent of children in the first century died by age six, [and] girls who made it past that age could expect to live only to their mid-twenties or thirties (men might, on average, live a decade longer). Two primary reasons explain early female mortality. First, the ancient diet generally lacked iron, which led to anemia and resulting miscarriages... or to diseases such as pneumonia, bronchitis, and emphysema that hit women hardest during menstruation and pregnancy. The second reason for women's early mortality is related to the first: women in antiquity commonly died during or shortly after childbirth.[62]

This verse regarding childbirth is one that has often been minimized or diminished as slightly mystical to many male commentators, but to any woman who is facing down her first childbirth experience (or even her tenth), it makes a great deal of sense. Even today, with all of the advances in modern medicine and technology, it's still the case in America that some healthy young women will die each year before, during, or soon after childbirth.[63] There is simply an unavoidable risk of death or serious injury during childbirth, and the fear from such an experience—or the anticipation of it—can be quite overwhelming. Although we should always place our trust and the outcome of a pregnancy into the hands of our heavenly Father, this experience of life-threatening danger is familiar to any mother.

Now suppose that you're a pregnant Ephesian woman. How afraid might you be, especially given the childbirth mortality statistics from this time period? What would you do for hope or comfort? For many women, the answer was simple: pray to Artemis. As Belleville notes, "An Artemis influence ... would also explain Paul's statement (v. 15) that 'women will be kept safe through childbirth'... for Artemis was the protector of women. Women turned to her for safe travel through the childbearing process.... [T]he maiden-goddess Artemis was invoked by women during labor."[64] This could very well explain Paul's comment. For some Christian women, particularly newer converts, the fear of childbirth could be so overwhelming that, much like the Israelites with their syncretistic worship of God and Baal, they may have strayed or returned to their former pagan goddess due to the risk of death or injury. Somewhat understandably—although heresy is not to be condoned—these young, uneducated women were petrified and using any means necessary in the hopes of survival. Paul was therefore encouraging them to "continue in faith, love and holiness with propriety."

But what of Paul's comment about being "saved" through childbirth? The Greek word that Paul used is *sōzō*, and throughout its 106 uses in the New Testament[65] it can mean both "save" and "kept safe." Because of the high maternal death rate during this period of history, some interpreters conclude that the "physical safety" sense of *sōzō* is implausible. However, as egalitarian Cynthia Westfall points out, the believer's prayer for physical healing is still encouraged in the book of James even though it doesn't always follow that the petition will be answered in the believer's lifetime (James 5:14–16).[66]

A negative outcome in *some* cases (e.g., death in childbirth or lack of healing) doesn't necessarily imply a negative outcome in *all* cases.

Others observe that *sōzō* is often used in a salvific sense elsewhere in the writings of Paul, and therefore it's certainly a possibility that Paul intends this meaning here in 1 Timothy 2:15. If this is so, then a glaring problem arises with a plain reading of the verse. Obviously, it cannot be the case that women are spiritually saved before God through the bearing of children, as that would make the gospel of grace into a gospel of works, specifically baby-bearing-based works. Since many women don't have the opportunity or capacity to bear children, this would significantly narrow the means by which women are capable of obtaining salvation and justification (i.e., right standing) before God. To avoid such an absurd result, Schreiner favors the spiritual application of the word *sōzō* because of the context in which the verse is mentioned, specifically false teaching and cults:

> If women are saved by bearing children, then does this not amount to salvation by works and contradict Pauline theology? Understanding the historical situation will aid us in answering this question. The false teachers, in trumpeting an over-realized eschatology, prohibited marriage and certain foods (1 Tim. 4:1–5). If they banned marriage, then they probably also criticized bearing children. Paul selected childbearing, then, as a specific response to the shafts from the false teachers.[67]

At this point in the debate, egalitarians understandably cry foul. In verse 15, Schreiner looks to the "historical situation" and infers that Paul's comments were made in response to the particular circumstances facing the Ephesian church, namely the infiltration of false teachers. In order to avoid reaching an otherwise false conclusion, Schreiner interprets this verse in a non-transcultural manner based on the relevant cultural factors involving a local heresy. But in the three *immediately preceding* verses, Schreiner takes an entirely opposite approach, even though the entire passage forms a conceptual and thematic whole. In the end, Schreiner significantly discounts cultural factors in verses 12–14 in order to support a plain reading of the text, while in the very next verse he interprets Paul according to cultural factors in order to avoid a plain reading of the text that could lead to an unfavorable interpretation. The question is once again why Schreiner engages in what seems like special pleading.

If a cultural lens isn't permissible for verses 12–14, why then would a cultural lens be so important in verse 15? As Sumner highlights, "The critical point is that it doesn't make sense to say that verse 15 *must* be alluding to a local heresy and that verses 13–14 *can't* be alluding to a local heresy. Thus I am not persuaded by any argument that says 1 Timothy 2:15 alone is situational while 1 Timothy 2:11–14 are universal."[68] Sumner's logic appears to be the most consistent in its application to this passage:

- "Both sides generally agree that 1 Timothy 2:8–10 alludes to a local situation." For example, it would be absurd to conclude that only men, not women, must pray with lifted hands.

- "Both sides generally agree that 1 Timothy 2:15 alludes to a local situation," that is, to a local heresy.

- Therefore, it's likely "that the verses sandwiched in between, namely 1 Timothy 2:11–14, also allude to a local situation, especially since both sides agree that all four verses, as traditionally understood, give rise to a number of" interpretive challenges.[69]

If the events surrounding the text are a strong influence on its content, as even Schreiner has conceded (i.e., "the circumstances addressed in New Testament documents affect the theme emphasized by the writers"), then it would seem to follow that 1 Timothy 2:11–14 should be interpreted in the same manner as the conceptually related verses that both precede and follow it. But as Sumner suggests, this isn't the approach taken by conservative complementarians, and a contextual indicator such as the created order doesn't seem adequate on its own to justify such a noticeably disjointed approach to interpretation.

One final point bears mentioning. Conservative complementarians like Schreiner assume that Paul is addressing gender roles in the public setting of the local church. This explains why Paul speaks of prayer (v. 8), modest dressing (v. 9), women learning quietly (v. 11), and women being prohibited from teaching or having authority (v. 12). But if the setting that Paul has in mind is a public gathering of Christians, why mention childbirth at all? As Westfall comments:

> Would "childbearing," which refers to the actual process of giving birth to a child, be an appropriate Pauline description for a woman's function in "a public worship context" or a woman's function in the Christian community? This is an important question, because most analyses of 1 Timothy 2:8–15 say that the passage provides instructions for public worship.[70]

Anyone remotely familiar with the biological process of childbirth should join me in hoping that this doesn't mean that childbirth ought to be a public experience shared by the wider Christian community. Counseling is expensive, and it might be widely needed if childbirth was incorporated into the public worship context. Surely even Paul (who was unmarried) must have known enough about human birth and reproduction to understand that childbirth was a *very* intimate experience, not a public one. The fact that Paul mentions such a private experience, one that has nothing to do with the public worship context, at the conclusion of this key passage could suggest that Paul has not been addressing the public worship context all along. Instead, he could have been addressing marriage, as suggested by the footnotes in the NIV which translate *gynē* as "wife" rather than "woman" in verses 11 and 12.

Conclusion

Thank you, dear reader, for bearing with me during this journey through the highlights of the scholarly debate over the most contested verses on women in ministry. As the reward for your diligence and tenacity, I hope that you feel more informed regarding what all the hullaballoo is about when 1 Timothy 2 is introduced into the discussion. Let us zoom out for a minute, though, and take stock of the fact that regardless of the meaning of *authenteō*, regardless of whether childbirth is mentioned in the context of the public worship service, and regardless of whether Ephesian women at every economic level were far more educated than the historical evidence suggests, these seven verses from Paul to Timothy are just strands of a much larger theological tapestry. Although the discussion has primarily focused on these verses, 1 Timothy 2:9–15 doesn't define and truncate the entire story for women in the body of Christ. As we continue our journey and discuss gifts later in this book, we will see that the scriptural imperative for women to faithfully use their God-given talents and abilities isn't so easily buried under the mountain of scholarship devoted to the meaning and application of 1 Timothy 2:9–15.

CHAPTER 6

A Woman's Role in the Church: Problems and Inconsistencies

> God's eternal law... has made the female sex subject to the authority of men. On this account all women are born, that they may acknowledge themselves inferior in consequence of the superiority of the male sex.
>
> —John Calvin

I was an English major in college, and when it comes to the topic of "roles," I can't help but think of Shakespeare's famous line from *As You Like It*:

All the world's a stage,
And all the men and women merely players;
They have their exits and their entrances,
And one man in his time plays many parts.
His acts being seven ages.[1]

Is this what comes to mind for you when you think of a "role," namely, a part that is only played for a time? (Actually, I *can* think of one other thing: rolls. Particularly the kind that are accompanied by words like "dinner" and "buttered.") Aside from bench-press and dead-lift competitions, women excel in every field, including theology. How then do we utilize gifted women and commission them to share the gospel, teach Scripture, develop new ministries, and gain the same sense of contentment in their work, regardless of their season of life? The current complementarian theology of "biblical womanhood" involving the "roles" of women has taken the non-biblical (i.e., not utilized in Scripture) word "role" that ordinarily references a temporary status and glossed it with a new meaning involving permanence. The result is to place the concept of "role" on the same immutable footing as gender. But surely this is a category mistake. It's certainly the case that our heavenly Father determined our genders. Male and female are not interchangeable; both are necessary and valuable in order to share the gospel to the ends of the earth and meet the needs of compassion in this hurting world. There is beauty, sacredness, wisdom, and purpose in the gender that God has given to each individual. Just as each ethnicity has intrinsic value from our Creator, so too does each gender. But gender and ethnicity are unchanging constants. The issue for egalitarians is that a "role" has a termination point in life; a role is not congenital and life-long. Unlike roles, which are temporary and often change, gender and ethnicity are given to strengthen the body of Christ and should be valued for their sacredness. They are irreplaceable, and our differences are what make us stronger ambassadors in this mission. Roles like teacher, single person, and child may come and go with time, but gender and ethnicity will not.

Unfortunately, insisting that roles are temporary, or that pas-

Women's Gifts, Women's Roles 91

sages like 1 Timothy 2:9–15 should *not* be elevated above others, is to risk heresy itself in the minds of conservative complementarians. They have widely adopted the term "role" to encapsulate their reading of 1 Timothy 2:9–15, and it's often combined with adjectives like "gender," "God-ordained," or "created." Based on their God-ordained gender roles, women are not to teach men or have authority over men. But here's the problem: the term "role" is not used in Scripture. As a result, a definitional question quickly arises. If gender is unchanging (i.e., immutable), as the Bible strongly suggests,[2] but roles are temporary, as the ordinary use of the term suggests, then in what biblical sense can women be said to have "roles"? In other words, can something truly be a "role" if it applies from first breath to last? Or is a "permanent role" a contradiction in terms?

Conservative complementarians are not unfamiliar with this argument, and they retort that a *permanent* subordination, or submission, of women to men is a valid example of a "role," because we have a similar example from the Trinity. In the Incarnation, Jesus the Son is functionally subordinate to God the Father,[3] but this in no way indicates that Jesus is somehow devalued by this.[4] As the saying goes, "Equal in value, but unequal in role." For conservative complementarians, women and men are on equal theological footing (e.g., God's image bearers) with one another, but intrinsically their roles require distinctions—leadership for men, on the one hand, and submission for women, on the other.

For egalitarians, what conservative complementarians propose is really just a new take on a very old idea: the world is inherently hierarchical, and women are always less than men. Cynthia Westfall doesn't mince words:

> [U]ntil very recently (ca. 1980s), traditional readings have assumed the ontological inferiority of women

through the entire history of interpretation, and it is implausible to think that an interpreter can effectively shed the foundational assumptions of the traditional [i.e., conservative complementarian] view and still coherently maintain the remainder of interpretations and applications virtually intact. Unless a scholar or interpreter assumes the superiority of men and inferiority of women as a presupposition for understanding the texts on gender, they cannot legitimately claim that his or her interpretation is in line with the traditions of Christianity.[5]

In terms of historical theology, Westfall is highlighting that for much of church history the complementarian view has been based on an assumption that women are *inferior as beings*, not in terms of their worth but in terms of their abilities, susceptibilities, and the like. Even Schreiner once seemed to think as much,[6] and Grudem appears to as well.[7]

This assumption is (formerly?) a key part of the complementarian argument. If you assume that God made men and women for specific gender-based roles, and Paul grounds his prohibition in 1 Timothy 2:12 (against women teaching or having authority) on Genesis and the created order, it seems to naturally follow (at least for complementarians) that women shouldn't teach or have authority because they're not as qualified as men. Otherwise, why have the prohibition at all? At least in a secular setting, common sense dictates that roles should be filled by those who are the most qualified. There's a reason that backup quarterbacks don't get much playing time for the New England Patriots—Tom Brady is on the team. Historically, a similar logic has applied in the church: Let the men teach and have authority because they're more qualified for the role *by virtue of their gender*. The connection seems inescapable: Women are *ontologically* (or in their being)[8] inferior individuals compared to men, at least with respect to certain abilities (e.g., teaching) and roles (e.g., leading).

Now, conservative complementarians understandably don't like this objection. What husband, son, or father with daughters wants to insinuate that the women in his life are somehow lesser than he? So, their response is often that the notion of a "role" shouldn't be confused with "personal worth." As conservative complementarian Raymond Ortlund explains, *"There is no necessary relation between personal role and personal worth.* Feminism denies this principle. Feminism insists that personal role and personal worth must go together, so that a limitation in role reduces or threatens personal worth."[9] But if "roles" are normally temporary, whereas personal worth is not, can we not challenge complementarians' assertion that personal worth and *permanent* personal roles are unrelated, without being labeled with the dreaded "F" word ("F" for "feminist" in this case)?

In response to conservative complementarians like Ortlund, egalitarian Rebecca Groothuis poses the following question in an essay on this topic:

> But what if it is not logically possible for the same person to be at once spiritually and ontologically equal *and* permanently, comprehensively and necessarily subordinate? What if this sort of subordination cannot truthfully be described as merely a "role" or "function" that has no bearing on one's inherent being or essence?[10]

In other words, what if the use of the word "role" is in fact inaccurate? What kind of "role" never ends or changes in life? Can it still be nothing more than a "role" if it's unalterable during the entire course of a person's life and possibly the eternity thereafter?

Again, conservative complementarians would say that this is possible because of the example of the Trinity. However, there is by no means an overwhelming consensus on this issue. In fact, many scholars would disagree with a Christological model in which Jesus the Son is *permanently* subordinated (or submissive) to God the Father rather than *temporarily* and functionally subordinated (or submissive) during the period of the Incarnation.[11] This is complicated theology, to be sure, but once again it's the case that educated and godly minds with a high view of Scripture can disagree with a key piece of the complementarian argument and for reasons having nothing to do with feelings or preference. If anything, the introduction of the Trinity into the middle of this debate reveals just how complex this topic can become, particularly when someone wishes to defend the claim that "roles" have no bearing on value.

Somewhat surprisingly, complementarians are internally divided about this issue of women's roles. First, consider the following statement from Piper, one I've already quoted elsewhere as an example of possible sexism and pride:

> The God-given sense of responsibility for leadership in a mature man will not generally allow him to flourish long under personal, directive leadership of a female superior. J. I. Packer suggested that "a situation in which a female boss has a male secretary" puts strain on the humanity of both. . . . And I would stress that this is not necessarily owing to male egotism, but to a natural and good penchant given by God.[12]

Second, and somewhat opposite, complementarian Craig Blomberg remarks with respect to 1 Corinthians 11:2–16 that:

> The passage does not address the issue of whether there are certain roles reserved for men in church, but it tacitly approves one key role for women—Spirit-filled preaching, which the contemporary church neglects to its detriment, inappropriately squelching the gifts of numbers of women and often damaging them psychologically in the process by telling them unbiblical things about what they can't or shouldn't do.[13]

Thus, where a conservative complementarian like Piper worries about the "strain on humanity" if a woman were to take a leadership position, a more centrist complementarian like Blomberg laments the loss suffered by the church and the resulting psychological harm to women when gender roles are wrongly addressed by the church. Ortlund may wish to believe that there is "*no necessary relation between personal role and personal worth*," but as his fellow complementarian suggests, the relation nevertheless seems quite real given the *psychological damage* to men if women lead (according to Piper) or to women who are stunted by gender-based roles (according to Blomberg). How can either gender be hurt if there is no relationship between personal role and personal worth?

When Metaphors Become Material

As you walk towards the confessional for the first time at roughly the age of seven, it's not uncommon for sweaty palms and shaking knees to reveal the inner fear of the great unknown. The gothic revival ceiling and décor surrounding you in the beautiful church help to fix your thoughts on higher things. A question is placed before each child: screen confessional or face-to-face? Do you have the courage to sit before the priest in the same room and look him in the eyes as you unburden your sins and receive your penance and absolution? Or do you choose the more cowardly route, one with a screen between the two of you to preserve some sense of anonymity? I have no memory of the confession I made to the priest when participating in my first Sacrament of Penance and Reconciliation in the early 1990s. However, the fear that was struck into me can still be easily recalled all these years later.

This was my experience at Our Lady Queen of Apostles parish in the heart of Hamtramck, a small city surrounded on all sides by the much larger city of Detroit, Michigan. Throughout much of the twentieth century Hamtramck was largely a Polish community and therefore very Roman Catholic, so much in fact that Pope John Paul II (who was Polish) visited the city in 1987. However, as automotive industry jobs moved away from the "Motor City," so too did the Polish immigrant families, including the younger generations. The Catholic school shut down a few years after I attended it, but along the way it had educated many young girls, including my Polish grandmother, who was a pupil there in the 1920s.

Although I attended the school more than seventy years after my grandmother did, one thing in particular never changed during that time: the access that we had to forgiveness from God, to communion, and to any other formal sacrament was always mediated by a priest. Fundamentally, Roman Catholicism consists of a *multilayered* church structure involving three levels of Christians: saints, the priesthood, and the laity (i.e., everyone else).[14] When I left the Roman Catholic Church and began attending a Protestant church at the age of eighteen, I had no expectation of ever again seeing something like this multilayered church structure outside of those Roman walls. However, much to my surprise, I would come to be proven quite wrong.

The apostle Paul wrote to the Galatians that it "is for freedom that Christ has set us free. Stand firm, then, and do not let yourselves be burdened again by a yoke of slavery" (Gal. 5:1). In his book on the atonement, theologian Leon Morris discusses the concept of "redemption" and highlights how we often forget Paul's admonition: "Mankind has a fiendish ingenuity in discovering ways of bringing itself into bondage. Paul's words are far from being out of date."[15] In Christ we have tremendous freedom, but we must heed Paul's warning lest we find ourselves in bondage once more. As Morris observes, this is indeed the regular pattern of human behavior: "Again and again it is not liberty in Christ which has characterized believers, but strict conformity to some new rule they have made or found."[16]

So let me speak plainly. We have already seen that the local church is described by conservative complementarians as a certain type of "family." In their view, just as fathers and mothers have different roles in the home, men and women have different roles in the church. However, while certain distinctions may exist in marriage, as suggested by Ephesians 5:21–33, the application of a marital analogy to the local church—with its men, women, children, college students, widows, singles, and everything else—ends up creating a *multilayered* church structure, only with two layers instead of three (like Roman Catholics). While a Protestant would very likely reject this notion of "levels" on theological grounds, in practice the conservative complementarian tendency to heavily emphasize gender-based roles (recall the "core values" of the Acts 29 network) serves to create two classes of kingdom citizens, one (the men) with more power, authority, and opportunities than the other (the women). Complementarians may balk at this notion, but this is precisely the implication of 1 Timothy 2:12 on a complementarian reading. If it's true for all time and all cultures that women shouldn't have authority over or opportunity to teach men, then it's nearly impossible to argue that within the church they don't also have less power, less authority, and fewer opportunities than men. The result is a two-level system of Christianity, including those who can fully exercise their gifts (men) in all circumstances and those who cannot (women). To egalitarians, this is understandably troubling. To complementarians like Schreiner and Piper, this is simply as it should be and part of God's wise order for the church.

Women on the Mission Field

I want to close with one final reality, this one rather shocking. One of the difficulties caused by excessive emphasis on *roles* (rather than *gifts*) arises when there are no clear roles to be filled in the foreign mission field. While many complementarians have expended (and will no doubt continue to expend) great energy to define the roles for men and women in the setting of Western and American evangelical churches—many of which are predominantly white—they have not done the same in the broader cross-cultural context. In reference to women leading and having authority in the mission field, Piper and Grudem surprisingly state the following:

> We do not wish to impede the great cause of world evangelization by quibbling over which of the hundreds of roles might correspond so closely to pastor/elder as to be inappropriate for a woman to fill. It is manifest to us that women are fellow workers in the gospel and should

strive side by side with men (Philippians 4:3; Romans 16:3, 12). For the sake of finishing the Great Commission in our day, we are willing to risk some less-than-ideal role assignments.[17]

Honestly, I almost dropped their book when I first read this. How can it be that they felt the need to compile a collection of essays totaling more than 500 pages in order to identify these role assignments on *American* soil, and all with a great deal of "quibbling," but when it comes to a foreign country they are quickly "willing to risk some less-than-ideal role assignments"? This smacks of the ends justifying the means. One can easily ask, why not risk some "less-than-ideal" role assignments here at home? What is it about working in other countries that turns the conservative complementarian zeal into an indifferent "meh"? If 1 Timothy 2:12 is as "transcultural" as complementarians like Piper say it is, then why does it seem to have geographic boundaries with regard to its application?

Now, I don't wish to be disrespectful toward these esteemed men who have devoted their lives to faithfully serving God, but the argument could be levied that these comments have negative racial or ethnic undertones. Honestly, I don't know their hearts, and so I will assume that this is not their intent. Even so, their fellow complementarian Blomberg asks a troubling question:

> Countless women from Western cultures have been permitted to preach, teach, evangelize, and in general lead evangelical ministries in non-Western countries—"on the mission field"—when their sending churches would never permit such practices "back home." Can this be anything other than a subtle racism that in essence says other cultures are so inferior that a double standard can be established for them?[18]

I appreciate Blomberg's candor in pointing out what seems to be a gross inconsistency in the approach of conservative complementarians. If a God-ordained hierarchy is meant to be present in the church, then so be it, but it should be reflected no matter where a church is located, whether abroad or "at home." Women have been instrumental in the advancement of the gospel on the mission fields throughout the world, and their success may be due in no small part to their decision to relocate internationally and thereby free themselves from white, American cultural roles that needlessly inhibit them from fulfilling the Great Commission.

Conservative complementarians may protest that the prohibitions in 1 Timothy 2:12 are anything but "needless," but it's hard to take serious the claim that gender roles are "God-ordained" when they can be conveniently tossed aside for the sake of missionary expediency. Again, if gender roles can be discarded abroad, then why not here as well? Perhaps egalitarians are onto something after all when they insist that the plain reading of 1 Timothy 2:12 need not apply in our present culture. If actions speak louder than words, then perhaps complementarians like Piper have already conceded the debate. Food for thought.

CHAPTER 7

Calling or Gifting? Biblical Definitions and Distinctions

"But surely in the case of distinguished people, you'd hear?"

"But they aren't distinguished—no more than anyone else. Don't you understand? The Glory flows into everyone, and back from everyone: like light and mirrors. But the light's the thing."

"Do you mean there are no famous men?"

"They are all famous. They are all known, remembered, recognised by the only Mind that can give a perfect judgment."

—C. S. Lewis, *The Great Divorce*

Then I heard the voice of the Lord saying, "Whom shall I send? And who will go for us?" And I said, "Here am I. Send me!"

—Isaiah 6:8

Few of us have taken Jesus' words to "lose our lives to find it" (Matt. 10:39) quite as literally as someone like Amy Carmichael, the famous female missionary to India. When Amy felt the call to become a missionary at a Keswick convention in 1887, she was immediately ready to board a ship headed to Asia. When Amy was asked what her life in India was like, she responded in her letter with the sentiment that "missionary life is simply a chance to die." Through the process of dying to herself and answering a "call," Amy founded a ministry to house and rescue hundreds of desperate children from the exploitation of the Hindu temple system. The rescued girls in particular were sexually abused by the temple priests, and both they and the resulting children that they bore had no hope of a future. This pattern of brokenness was shattered by the radical love of Jesus that Amy brought with her to India.

An experience of a call like Amy's sounds so powerful and majestic because it resonates deeply with our own personal cries to embrace lives of meaning, purpose, and value. The notion of "calling" cuts through layers of identity to the very heart of our desires. Once we have answered the call into relationship with God the Father through Jesus Christ and the Holy Spirit (Matt. 9:13; 22:14), and the process of sanctification has thereafter begun,[1] we desire to know more: about God, about the Word, and about the way in which we fit into the body of Christ that has been given the privilege of sharing the gospel with the world (Matt. 28:18–20).

While these desires are noble, the hunger to fulfill one's "calling" and live in a significant manner also comes with the risk of self-centeredness. I suspect that deep within many hearts, including my own, is also a self-focused drive or desire to be found noteworthy or exceptional in some way. Crack open *Guinness World Records 2017* and take a gander at how far people will go in order to claim a title—almost any title—

that no one else can. Consuming an airplane piece by piece, living with foot-long nails on each finger, shipping in tons of sand to sculpt a sandcastle that will be erased with the wind and rain—these all sing the same refrain. God has set eternity in the human heart (Eccl. 3:11), and so we naturally want to leave behind some kind of legacy that carves our names into the memories of those who survive us, even if only for a time. Although Christians should be entirely set free from this sort of thinking, because our names have been written in the Book of Life (Phil. 4:3) and we are co-heirs with Christ who will inherit everything (Rom. 8:17), we still need to be on our guard against this desire for significance clouding the discussion of ministry, gifts, and calling.

What Is the Definition of "Calling"?

In his book *The Call*, Os Guinness very helpfully differentiates between the universal, primary call to Christ and a secondary vocational call:

> A special calling refers to those tasks and missions laid on individuals through a direct, specific, supernatural communication from God. Ordinary calling, on the other hand, is the believer's sense of life-purpose and life-task in response to God's primary call, "follow me," even when there is no direct, specific, supernatural communication from God about a secondary calling. In other words, ordinary calling can be seen in our responsibility to exercise a high degree of "capitalist-style" enterprise about how we live our lives. For example, the servants in Jesus' parable of the talents and [minas] were assessed according to how they "got on with it" when the master was away. In this sense no follower of Christ is without

a calling, for we all have an original calling even if we do not all have a later, special calling.[2]

I do have to point out something important in response to this definition of "calling." While it's true that secondary callings (i.e., "special callings") are recorded in Scripture, they are rare. In fact, they are *exceptionally* rare. Christian apologist Greg Koukl has studied the use of the word "call" in the New Testament, and he observes that the word has four major uses other than "referred to," "beckoned," or "named." His observations are insightful:

- The general call is an invitation to faith—the call to salvation. Both *kletos* (Matt. 22:14) and *kaleo* (Matt. 9:13) are used for this purpose.

- The "effective call" is used mostly by Paul. This refers to God's work of bringing a person to faith and the holy life they are to live. "The called" are sinners who have responded in faith to the general call of God (Acts 2:39; 1 Cor. 7:15; Phil. 3:14; 1 Tim. 6:12).

- Some are "called" by receiving special spiritual gifts. The main example is Paul, who was "called" to be an apostle (Rom. 1:1; 1 Cor. 1:1).

- The word "call" can refer to supernatural revelation. However, "in only three instances out of 218 uses of a form of the word *kaleo* [or 1.38% of the time] does the writer refer to specific, supernatural, individualized revelation: [1] Paul and Barnabas' first missionary journey (Acts 13:2); [2] [a] [v]ision calling Paul to preach in Macedonia (Acts 16:10); [and] [3] [o]f Abraham [Hebrews 11:8.]"[3]

All who follow Jesus and confess him as Lord have a *general* call. However, as Koukl's research demonstrates, while it's certainly not impossible that someone might receive a "special calling," the record from Scripture suggests that such an event is rare indeed. Therefore, based on passages such as Romans 12:6, 1 Corinthians 12:7, Ephesians 4:11-12, and 1 Peter 4:10-11, Koukl's suggestion is that we should expect God to distribute ministry by *gifting* rather than by *calling*.[4]

Furthermore, the supernatural element of "the call," as the term is most commonly used in contemporary Christian culture today with respect to *specific* ministries (e.g., "called to be a pastor"), is simply not the same as its New Testament relative. Unless those who use the term are referring to an audible voice or vision from God in connection with their special or individualized calling,[5] the "calling" itself is not supernatural or divinely directed in the same way that it was for Paul and the Old Testament prophets, and therefore it doesn't fit into any of the four biblical categories identified by Koukl.

A Calling or a Gifting?

Now, at this point you might be tempted to throw up your hands in exasperation. I realize that for many the notion of "calling" is deeply felt and important, and I honestly mean no offense at this suggestion, nor do I want to cast any doubt on a deeply felt call. However, studying how the word "call" is used in the New Testament reveals that the modern church uses this biblical term in a manner not supported by the text. In other words, the concept of being "called" to a specific type of ministry is actually more of a lexical adaptation of modern Christian culture, not a clearly taught biblical doctrine. I was shocked myself when I first read Koukl and the books on which his materials are based,[6] but the evidence for the modern notion of a personal or individualized or special "calling"—absent supernatural direction from God—just isn't there. While this might sound like nitpicking, I think it's helpful to use biblical words in biblical ways. Ultimately, I suspect that what many feel is a "calling" is really a combination of God-given interest, passion, and gifting.

Piper actually is a good example of this. He describes his own experience of sensing his "call" in the following manner:

> Do you find this work desirable? Is your desire growing? Is it reaching the point of irresistibility? That is what happened for me on October 14, 1979 when I was struggling with whether to stay a professor at a college or whether to be a pastor. And all I knew to say was that at about midnight that night, it became irresistible after years of brewing.[7]

While only some Christians will experience a supernatural "special call" in the form of an audible or internal voice from God, Scripture indicates that *all* Christians are equipped with gifts and are thereby able to joyfully serve the world and redeem the days. I make this distinction because many egalitarian authors, when discussing the legitimacy of women utilizing their gifts in additional church settings, often lump "calling" and "gifting" together when presenting their case. However, I believe it's more helpful—and truer to the use of language in Scripture—for egalitarians to distinguish the two and stake their case for greater inclusion of female teachers on the multitude of verses that pertain to spiritual gifts. For example, egalitarian Gordon Fee writes:

> To begin with gender rather than gifts and calling simply puts the emphasis at the wrong place, especially for the

new covenant people of God, where there is no longer any priesthood (at least not as part of biblical revelation!). Further, God explicitly announced that he would pour out his Spirit on *all* people for prophetic ministry (Joel 2:28–29), where "all" is explicitly defined in categories of men/women, slave/free and young/old.[8]

Although Fee and other egalitarians combine gifts and calling together, I would contend that the focus should primarily be on gifts which, unlike the subjective concept of "calling," are far more tangible, outwardly identifiable by others, possibly more permanent, and more objective in nature. (Even though Romans 11:29 states that "God's gifts and call are irrevocable," the use of "call" seems to be in the primary sense of Koukl's "effective call" rather than a vocational one.)

While no one particularly likes to talk about this aspect of Christian culture in America, I feel it may be necessary in order to address a common source of confusion. Over the years I've encountered numerous Christians who have said that they "felt called to x" one day, only to later sense that they "felt called to y" sometime not long after. I don't think this experience is uncommon, as some of my Christian friends have observed (or exhibited) this same behavior. Such shifts in direction can easily generate confusion, both for the Christian trying to discern his or her "calling" as well as the friends and family members invested in this person's life. What is the source of this confusion? If x and y are fundamentally different or incompatible callings, then how is it that God would change his mind so radically and so quickly?[9] Because proposing that God is confused or bad at giving directions seems to border on heresy, I tend to think the confusion and mind-changing can be properly attributed to the human side of the equation. In other words, the confusion seems to arise when we forget that calling is very often, although certainly not always, more general in nature and less like directional life coordinates beamed down from heaven.

The general calling is to love the Lord, love others, and share the gospel (Matt. 22:37–40; 28:18–20). As both Guinness and Koukl highlight, if you look beyond this or overemphasize the search for a personal vocational "calling," too much self-analysis and introspection can be paralyzing. If we are consistently focused on the "special" calling that we must discover in order to be in the "center of God's will," then we may miss the needed good works that already await us in this present season (Eph. 2:10). God can certainly do anything, including provide particular individuals with a supernatural special calling, but as a matter of practice, and based on the biblical narrative as a whole, it seems that believers should be active in the present and look to God for wisdom and gifts (1 Cor. 12:31). The Lord's brother said it well: "If any of you lacks wisdom, you should ask God, who gives generously to all without finding fault, and it will be given to you. . . . Do not merely listen to the word, and so deceive yourselves. Do what it says" (James 1:5, 22).

To quickly recap the last two chapters, I have argued that conservative complementarians are wrong to analyze the issue of women in ministry using the notion of *permanent* gender roles, as the concept is not found in Scripture and seems to be a contradiction in terms. I have also argued that egalitarians are mistaken in basing their position on the notion of "calling," as this term, while found in the Bible, in most cases has a general rather than an individual application. Both sides of the debate have selected terms that they find helpful, but the biblical study of "roles" and "calling," for the reasons I have laid out, is unlikely to provide much insight. In the next chapter, I conclude with a concept that *is* well-attested in Scripture, unambiguous, and provides clear answers: gifting.

CHAPTER 8

Developing Women's Gifts: A Biblical and Moral Imperative

Full many a gem of purest ray serene,
The dark unfathom'd caves of ocean bear:
Full many a flower is born to bush unseen,
And waste its sweetness on the desert air.

—Thomas Gray,
Elegy Written in a Country Churchyard

Each of you should use whatever gift you have received to serve others, as faithful stewards of God's grace in its various forms.

—1 Peter 4:10

ONE LATE SUMMER afternoon, I hosted a small meeting of female leaders to discuss upcoming women's ministry events at our local church. The last item on the list that day was one that I thought would be an enjoyable topic of discussion: the upcoming women's retreat for our local church. Another woman and I had planned the previous women's retreat two years earlier—the first and only retreat that had taken place in the church's seven-year history—and I was eager to attempt another one.

As soon as the topic was raised, our (female) leader promptly took the helm and politely declared that the topic and content of the retreat had already been determined by the (male) senior pastor and that a particular book by a female complementarian author would be the sole information covered at the retreat. Even though there was clearly (and rather unexpectedly) no invitation for me to offer suggestions, questions, or comments on the issue, I proceeded to ask if it would still be possible to include a component of leadership development or spiritual gift testing in addition to the book content. Then something strange happened. As soon as I asked my question, our leader's disposition sharply changed. Her usually warm, sunny, and kind demeanor disappeared, and her face turned to stone. Although I had not called into question the reliability of Scripture, the historicity of the Gospels, or the reality of the virgin birth, I may as well have done so given her terse response to my question: "No."

Looking back, I suppose I should have seen this coming. Conservative complementarian theology had become so deeply imbedded in the foundations of this local church's culture that even the *attempt* to encourage women's gifts was seen as a borderline mutiny. Two years prior, when organizing the previous (and only) women's retreat, I had invited a long-time female staff worker with InterVarsity Christian Fellowship (IVCF) to devote a few hours during the retreat to women's gift development. Over time, as the church became more involved with the Acts 29 network and increasingly open about its growing conservative complementarian ideology, the gift development component became a deeply unpopular idea.

Women's Gifts, Women's Roles

I later learned that at the time of my backyard conversation over tea, the gift development experience had already fostered deep suspicion. Although the vast majority of the content for the first retreat had focused on evangelism training, allocating any component of time for women to review and evaluate their spiritual gifts and goals was deemed to be potentially divisive. Now, in my own back garden, this godly, Jesus-loving woman with whom I had labored for years as a fellow elder's wife, this friend with whom I had memorized Romans 12 in a Bible study for church leaders, was insisting—as a matter of unwritten church policy—that women who possess the maturity for leadership should be content with studying only Scripture and not straying into any discussion about evaluating spiritual gifts. At this moment, I realized that no matter how much I loved the people of this local church community, there would likely never be a meaningful chance to identify and encourage the gifts of women without encountering blockades at nearly every turn.

Disputed Versus Undisputed Passages

In all honesty, I share this story with regret, not to vent or cast aspersions. I was deeply saddened by this encounter, and when I reflect upon it I still feel some sadness. But here is the point of my winding story (there is one I think): Even if one accepts all of the *disputed* passages on this topic as conservative complementarians understand them, without taking into account the cultural setting and context that shape or determine meaning, and transport them directly into the twenty-first century church structure, women can *still* be held accountable by a large number of *undisputed* passages that speak to the development, cultivation, and application of spiritual gifts. And yet, at this church, and likely many others as well that accept or share "core values" similar to those of the Acts 29 network, focusing too much on the development and exercise of women's gifts can be seen, rightly or wrongly, as trending toward (or even embracing) the "evangelical feminism" that complementarians like Grudem and Piper so vehemently abhor.

Why is this so? Why have a few sharply contested passages, such as those covered in chapter 5, not only come to define the roles of one-half or more of a church community's members, but also limited their conduct in such a manner as to practically discourage any development that is not perceived as "traditional" enough? Even centrist complementarians have identified the need for and high value in using and developing spiritual gifts as a general rule. Blomberg provides the following key test for any church or male leader:

> *Once you have decided, as best as you can understand it, what Scripture does permit women to do, can any reasonably objective observer of your church and your ministry quickly recognize you are bending over backwards to encourage and nurture women in these roles?* If not, then you can't possibly be obeying Scripture adequately, *even on your interpretation of it.* Interestingly, over the years, I have had a number of outspoken egalitarian women, some of them well known in evangelical circles, confide in me privately and tell me that if complementarians would just do this much consistently, they could live with the remaining areas of disagreement and even stop lobbying for further privilege.[1]

Even if conservative complementarians are correct, disputed passages like 1 Timothy 2:9–15 don't diminish the importance of building up the entire body of Christ and encouraging *all*

Christians with spiritual gifts to make the whole body stronger. No doubt with an unspoken complementarian qualification, even Schreiner would agree:

> Paul's main point [in Romans 12:3–8] is that those who have such gifts should devote themselves to the gift that they have received. Those who serve to service, those who teach to teaching, and those who exhort to exhorting.... Once believers have identified their gifts they should strive to excel in the gifts they have been given and devote themselves to the body by exercising those gifts. For example, teachers are not exempted from serving others, from rendering financial assistance, from showing mercy, and so on. Nonetheless, teachers should especially concentrate on studying so that their teaching is effective.[2]

Similarly, complementarian Douglas Moo would as well: "Paul is concerned that those who have the gift of teaching faithfully use that gift."[3] If this is true for men in the body of Christ who have gifts, then how could it not also be true for women? Certainly, conservative complementarians will cite passages such as 1 Timothy 2:9–15, which we have already explored in depth. But two things stand out. First, we have also seen that 1 Timothy 2:9–15 is an *unclear* passage, one that has sharply divided theologians and New Testament scholars. Second, other passages that stress the importance of utilizing spiritual gifts, such as Romans 12:3–8, 1 Corinthians 12:4–11, and 1 Peter 4:10–11, are both *clear* (as even complementarians seem to admit) and *unqualified* in their language, imposing no direct or indirect gender-based limits on the broad exercise of women's gifts.

The following example illustrates the predicament facing

women. Mary Kassian, a professor of women's studies at the same seminary as Schreiner, wrote the following in a recent Desiring God[4] article:

> Arguably, because I am a gifted teacher, I could do a better job of interpreting the text and delivering the sermon than many church-fathers do. But that would miss the point. It's not about competence. God created the family and, in the family, men are supposed to be the dads and women are supposed to be the moms. It's not a question of who is better at it or more gifted. Male-female roles are neither identical nor interchangeable.[5]

Kassian goes on to provide her personal eight-factor test for deciding which speaking engagements she will accept and which she will decline if it may involve teaching with men present.[6] I certainly appreciate her candor in admitting that this does create a predicament for women who possess the gift of teaching. At least she doesn't try to pass it off like it's no big deal. However, it *is* a big deal—a *very* big deal. The complementarian logic that a woman's role in the church is not about competence or gifting, but rather God's hierarchy involving "dad-mom" dynamics, seems to undermine much of what the New Testament has to say about the use of gifts.

Gifting: A Matter of Competence

Consider again what Kassian writes: "I am a gifted teacher, I could do a better job of interpreting the text and delivering the sermon.... But that would miss the point. It's not about competence." Come again? Certainly, such logic would sound utterly confused to any HR manager or chief operating officer.

But is this true even *within* the church? Consider next some of the following excerpts from the New Testament epistles:

- "The eye cannot say to the hand, 'I don't need you!' And the head cannot say to the feet, 'I don't need you!' On the contrary, those parts of the body that seem to be weaker are indispensable.... Now you are the body of Christ, and each one of you is a part of it. And God has placed in the church first of all apostles, second prophets, third teachers, then miracles, then gifts of healing, of helping, of guidance, and of different kinds of tongues" (1 Cor. 12:21–22, 27–28).

- "Each of you should use whatever gift you have received to serve others, as faithful stewards of God's grace in its various forms. If anyone speaks, they should do so as one who speaks the very words of God. If anyone serves, they should do so with the strength God provides, so that in all things God may be praised through Jesus Christ" (1 Pet. 4:10–11).

- "We have different gifts, according to the grace given to each of us. If your gift is . . . teaching, then teach" (Rom. 12:6–7).

I will have more to say on these passages shortly. For now, notice the seeming contradiction between what Kassian writes and what Paul and Peter wrote centuries ago. God has scattered different gifts among people throughout his church, and we cannot say to any one of them "I don't need you." Rather, each of us should use our gifts "to serve others" as a "faithful steward." If that gift is teaching, "then teach." This is *not* the language of "It's not about competence." Competence is an indication of gifting, and so if anything these verses indicate that it *is* about competence. Romans 12 essentially says, "If you're competent, go exercise that competency—i.e., use your gifts—for the benefit of the church." Once again, even Schreiner takes this broad view: "Once believers have identified their gifts they should strive to excel in the gifts they have been given and devote themselves to the body by exercising those gifts."[7]

Kassian might respond that these verses should be interpreted in light of the transcultural prohibitions contained in passages like 1 Timothy 2:9–15. But why didn't Paul or Peter make reference to such restrictions? Elsewhere, Paul is certainly not shy about noting rules that he lays down "in all the churches" (1 Cor. 7:17). So why favor 1 Timothy 2 over these three passages (or the others like them)? Why does a passage as contested, debated, and contextually nuanced as 1 Timothy 2:9–15 override multiple, clear, and unqualified exhortations to use your gifts to the fullest for the glory of God?

Every analogy has points of similarity between the things being compared, but it also has points of dissimilarity. What is true in the context of a nuclear family is not always true in the context of a local church. If anything, Kassian seems to press the analogy too far, as her description of "moms and dads" is more fitting for a commune than for a church community. As egalitarians Mimi Haddad and Alvera Mickelsen comment:

> [T]ake 1 Corinthians 12, where we find clear teaching regarding God's gifts to all his people. God gives his gifts as he chooses, and all believers are to use their gifts for the good of the "body," his church. There is no suggestion that men get "leadership gifts" and women get "service gifts." Such passages are clear and do not need abstract theological language to explain them. They fit the Genesis

account of men and women alike being created in the image of God and sharing responsibility for God's world.[8]

More to the point, although there are passages that mention the "household of God" (1 Tim. 3:15; 1 Pet. 4:17), it doesn't seem that Priscilla (Acts 18), Junia (Rom. 16:7),[9] or Phoebe (Rom. 16:1) were trying to become men (or dads) by using their gifts for the glory of God. To insist otherwise would be to set up an egalitarian strawman and then demolish it with a puff of breath. In fact, none of the egalitarian writers that I have studied have advocated for fully interchangeable roles in this manner; thoughtful egalitarian scholars recognize the clear truth of Scripture that men and women *are* different in important ways. However, contrary to Kassian, they would insist that gifting should be considered a much more relevant qualification for teaching than biological gender alone. For the body of Christ to be edified, teaching *is* "a question of who is better at it or more gifted."

Recall Paul's words in 1 Timothy 2:12: "I do not permit a woman to teach or to assume authority over a man." With regard to her eight-factor test, Kassian writes, "I have found that as I get older I have more freedom to instruct younger men as a mother instructs her sons." But why couldn't a "church-mother" teach in a public setting if she is already gifted to do so, both with younger men and within her own household? Wouldn't her unique perspective and voice offer something to the entire congregation, even if it was only in an occasional or more informal way? Doesn't Kassian teach men when they read her written words? Should a visitor to her website have to attest to being female so as not to "controvert God's created order"?[10] I suppose she wouldn't have to worry about that too much, though, for in the conservative complementarian paradigm a godly man who takes 1 Timothy 2:12–14 seriously would never have a reason to pick up a book authored by a woman in the first place.

Arbitrary Rules

Such questions are not the mere grumblings of frustrated egalitarian women. Complementarians Robert Saucy and Judith TenElshof highlight how arbitrary it is to allow women to teach men in some contexts but not others:

> Another distinction in relation to women's teaching is similarly questionable. In this view, women are prohibited from publicly teaching with men present, but are encouraged to teach through writing, including scholarly scriptural studies. It is interesting to note that the writings of some women have significantly influenced the thought even of some men who reject their public teaching of men. It is difficult to understand why, if men can learn from women through writing, they cannot learn from them through oral teaching.[11]

These sorts of inconsistencies, which are not uncommon in complementarian churches, provide a good illustration of elevating form over substance. Again, recall Paul's statement in 1 Timothy 2:12: "I do not permit a woman to teach or to assume authority over a man." If conservative complementarians are correct in claiming that this amounts to a transcultural principle prohibiting women from teaching men, why are they comfortable with the fact that "the writings of some women have significantly influenced the thought even of some men"? Why do they disfavor speech but not written words, even when the content is the same? Is it because they don't want to claim that men shouldn't read books written by women? If so,

Women's Gifts, Women's Roles

isn't that just caving to cultural pressure? My background is in regulatory compliance, and I can say with confidence that what Saucy and TenElshof describe—permitting women to engage in writing but not public speaking—feels like the sort of loophole that only a clever attorney would be proud of. My husband is a corporate and securities attorney, and he agreed that we would be very proud to discover such a loophole in a regulation.

As Blomberg notes, "pastor" is a gift, not an office in the church like elder or deacon. Moreover, many local churches fail to see the importance of including women in their plans:

> Here it is helpful to distinguish spiritual gifts from church offices.... At heart, the term "pastor" simply means "shepherd"—one who comes alongside one or more other people to care for them in any of a myriad of ways.... [I]t then becomes crucial to have gifted, godly women in all of the remaining levels of leadership. And the male pastor or board of elders needs regularly to consult these women in all matters of significance for the life of the church; how else can he or they function as servant leaders, implementing what is best for the whole congregation, including the women? When one recognizes the biblical restrictions on women exclusively to involve an *office* (or specific position or role), it becomes clear there are no *tasks* or ministry gifts they cannot or should not exercise—including preaching, teaching, evangelizing, pastoring, and so on.[12]

While egalitarians would deny that restrictions on offices apply today, they would wholeheartedly affirm Blomberg's other conclusions. The church *needs* women to exercise their gifts.

Suppose then that a woman desires to obtain a seminary

degree in order to cultivate and better utilize her gifts as a full-time pastor at a local church. Unfortunately, her employment options after graduation will be much more limited than those of men, also leaving her with fewer avenues for repaying the debt incurred from the cost of schooling. Generally speaking, there are only certain denominations that would hire a woman for a position that requires a graduate-level seminary degree, and many more that would not hire a woman for any such position. While this system is defended as necessary based upon God-ordained gender roles, it can easily become one that discourages women from practically developing anything that isn't seen as profitable for bake-offs, rearing children, and service roles. It's clear that this is not the direct intention of these men who love Jesus and seek to serve him and his church on earth, but it's the natural outworking. As Schreiner writes with respect to 1 Timothy 2:15, "a woman should not violate her role by teaching or exercising authority over a man; instead, she should take her proper role as a mother of children."[13] If a woman's "proper role" is mothering children, why waste time on other side endeavors that might involve a different role? If women are discouraged from teaching in any context that includes both genders, then almost inevitably it seems that their ability to develop and exercise their gifts—teaching, preaching, pastoring, etc.—will be practically limited in a number of ways. When this happens, everyone in the church loses.

In a recent address, complementarian author and speaker Jen Wilkin made the rather striking comment that "women understand powerlessness in a unique way."[14] While this doesn't sound like a ringing endorsement for developing women's gifts, it reveals one way that the gender differences can enhance the conversation on growing as disciples of Christ. Many are powerless in the world and lack a voice, and therefore teachers with a unique female perspective that understands powerlessness, as well as different approaches that incorporate more relational content, can only serve to sharpen the church. Since women are often more adept at making personal connections, they can serve in different ways than their male counterparts. In fact, on an anatomical level, women have more connections between the lobes of their brains than men do:

> Essentially, gray matter is like the computing power of the brain (where the actual processing and functioning is done) while white matter is like the network cables that connect the computers for speed, allow them to work together, and send signals from one computer to the next. Well, women have more white matter in their brain's superhighway than [men] do; while men have more gray matter. Neither is better or worse, but each leads to different ways of working through thoughts and emotions.[15]

One of the benefits of God's design is that women experience a quicker connection between the heart and the mind. Or as TenElshof writes, "Since women have more connections between the two sides of the brain, they may have... [the] ability to integrate the experience of emotions with the rational process of analytical thought."[16] Women often, though of course not always, approach a topic or lesson in a different manner than men, and this greater connection between the rational and the emotional could prove to be invaluable to every generation. Perhaps this is the true essence of the complementary nature between men and women. Such unity in diversity reflects the very nature of our triune God: "So God created mankind in his own image, in the image of God he created them; male and female he created them" (Gen. 1:27).

Talents and Minas: The Morality of Utilizing Gifts

The parable of the talents (Matt. 25:14–30) and the minas (Luke 19:11–27) both emphasize a similar fundamental lesson about gifts: use them! Use them and trust our heavenly Father for the resulting outcome, because God is indeed trustworthy. While the last verse in the parable of the minas (Luke 19:27) could be intended as hyperbole, the consequences of hiding or not using your gifts from God are quite severe:

> [11] While they were listening to this, he went on to tell them a parable, because he was near Jerusalem and the people thought that the kingdom of God was going to appear at once. [12] He said: "A man of noble birth went to a distant country to have himself appointed king and then to return. [13] So he called ten of his servants and gave them ten minas. 'Put this money to work,' he said, 'until I come back.'
>
> [14] "But his subjects hated him and sent a delegation after him to say, 'We don't want this man to be our king.'
>
> [15] "He was made king, however, and returned home. Then he sent for the servants to whom he had given the money, in order to find out what they had gained with it.
>
> [16] "The first one came and said, 'Sir, your mina has earned ten more.'
>
> [17] "'Well done, my good servant!' his master replied. 'Because you have been trustworthy in a very small matter, take charge of ten cities.'
>
> [18] "The second came and said, 'Sir, your mina has earned five more.'
>
> [19] "His master answered, 'You take charge of five cities.'

²⁰ "Then another servant came and said, 'Sir, here is your mina; I have kept it laid away in a piece of cloth. ²¹ I was afraid of you, because you are a hard man. You take out what you did not put in and reap what you did not sow.'

²² "His master replied, 'I will judge you by your own words, you wicked servant! You knew, did you, that I am a hard man, taking out what I did not put in, and reaping what I did not sow? ²³ Why then didn't you put my money on deposit, so that when I came back, I could have collected it with interest?'

²⁴ "Then he said to those standing by, 'Take his mina away from him and give it to the one who has ten minas.'

²⁵ "'Sir,' they said, 'he already has ten!'

²⁶ "He replied, 'I tell you that to everyone who has, more will be given, but as for the one who has nothing, even what they have will be taken away. ²⁷ But those enemies of mine who did not want me to be king over them—bring them here and kill them in front of me.'"[17]

While it's important to keep in mind that this is a parable and not intended for a literal translation into application—no one is advocating for the execution of those who "bury" their gifts—it's no less a powerful insight into the high value placed upon any heaven-sent gift. The similar parable in Matthew 25 uses the word *talanton* instead of *mina*, and while both were ancient units of currency, the modern word "talent" comes from *talanton*. The fact that gifts and talents and abilities are all in view, rather than mere economic resources, comes from the nature of the reward: "Because you have been trustworthy in a very small matter, take charge of ten cities" (Luke 19:17), and "You have been faithful with a few things; I will put you in charge of many things" (Matt. 25:21). God has no need of Warren Buffets or economic *wunderkinds*; his kingdom doesn't run on money. Rather, he entrusts his "wealth" to us (Matt. 25:14; cf. 1 Cor. 12:11) in many forms, and he expects that we will use our God-given resources wisely and promises to reward us for doing so:

> Probably we should understand the talents to represent all the working capital that God entrusts to His disciples. To limit the significance of talents to ... spiritual gifts, natural abilities, the gospel, opportunities for service, money, or whatever ... limits the scope of what Jesus probably intended. All of these things constitute what God has given His servants to use for His glory.[18]

It's therefore not merely a missed opportunity if we don't use our gifts for the glory of God. Rather, it's *sin*, a moral failure, one that reflects a deeper problem involving a lack of trust in the very Gift-giver himself:

> This slave evidently felt that his master would not share many of the rewards of his labor with him, if he proved successful, but would punish him severely if he failed.... He ignored his responsibility to his master and his obligation to discharge his duty. Moreover, he showed no love for his master, whom he blamed, attempting thereby to cover up his own failure.... Rather than commending this slave, his master gave him a scathing condemnation. Instead of being "good and faithful," he was "wicked" and "lazy." To be lazy is to be unfaithful.[19]

Conservative complementarian Don Carson summarizes the lesson well: "Grace never condones irresponsibility; even those given less are obligated to use and develop what they have."[20] Each one of us is accountable for the application and use of any and all gifts that we have received from God. Unfaithfulness, obligation, duty, responsibility: these are words loaded with deep and significant moral implications, and we dare not ignore them.

The lesson of the parables is so important because Scripture also teaches that we cannot say to any part of the body of Christ, "I don't need you" (1 Cor. 12:21). We are all relevant and valuable to the achievement of God's holy mission and seeing it through; no one can be left out.[21] Certainly more than pride or a fixation on "rights," this awareness of how important it is to utilize our gifts—and the moral consequences for failing to do so—is what I think really motivates egalitarians. As Westfall writes:

> Any believer who either fails to do what God intends or fails in doing it for the right reasons with holy character will pay a profound price in the eschatological judgment. This is exactly the point of Jesus's parable of the talents in Matthew 25:14–30. Whatever believers have received from God must be invested in order to benefit him and accomplish his purposes, and if they refuse to do so, the consequences are severe. For Paul, the default place for investment was in the church, and yet many women have been restricted from using the majority of the gifts listed [in Paul's letters] in the church because they involve speaking or leadership.... Men are saying to gifted women, "I have no need of you," which is a violation of Scripture (1 Cor. 12:21–26). Consequently, women who show themselves to be gifted in areas other than service, showing mercy, giving, and faith are prey to being underutilized, misused, or even treated with hostility.[22]

Consequently, limiting the use of women's gifts out of a desire for men's comfort, such as Piper suggests with his recommendation against "offend[ing] a man's... sense of responsibility and leadership,"[23] shouldn't be done casually. The spiritual consequences of limiting the use of another's gifts could very well include quenching the Holy Spirit, reducing that person's reward in heaven,[24] dishonoring the God we love, and denying needed blessing to multitudes.

Using the Unclear to Read the Clear

To quickly recap, we have already seen that the interpretation of 1 Timothy 2:9–15, which is behind so much of the limiting of women's gifts, is hotly debated. Moreover, complementarians like Blomberg admit that their viewpoint *could be wrong*, in which case egalitarians would be right. Finally, the necessity and importance of using gifts and talents and abilities for the glory of God is not lost upon *either* side of the debate. Consequently, I believe that conservative complementarians like Grudem, Piper, and Schreiner begin with the wrong starting point with respect to women's gifts. Rather than follow the hermeneutical approach of reading *unclear* passages (e.g., 1 Timothy 2:9–15) in light of *clear* passages on gifts (e.g., Romans 12:3–8), it seems that they have done the opposite, reading the prohibitions of 1 Timothy 2:12–14 into all of the various *unqualified* passages on gifts. Not only that, but as we saw in chapter 4, they have even elevated their interpretation of an unclear passage to the level of essential doctrine! Westfall nicely summarizes their mistake:

> The passage on spiritual gifts in 1 Corinthians 12–14 gives the most detail about the gifts, including their variety and functions in the church, and reflects the Holy

Spirit's primary role in the distribution of these gifts. Ephesians 4:7–13 shows that there is a direct relationship between the gifts provided by God and positions of leadership and ministry in the church, including the list of apostles, prophets, evangelists, pastors, and teachers in verse 11.... [A]n interpretation of the prohibitions against women in 1 Timothy 2:12 has taken priority over their exercise of most of the spiritual gifts outlined in Ephesians 4:11, Romans 12:1–8, and 1 Corinthians 12:28. The interpretation of 1 Timothy 2:12 functions as an a priori assumption that operates as a hermeneutical grid over these and other passages.... I question [the use of 1 Timothy 2:12] in interpreting Romans 12:1–8 on spiritual gifts because the Roman church could not have used it as an interpretive grid. Furthermore, I repeat that we should not base a doctrine on one verse, we should not base a doctrine on a verse or passage that carries interpretive problems, and we should give preference to the clearer passage in Romans and let it assist us in interpreting the less clear passage in 1 Timothy.[25]

Rather than undermining "biblical fidelity," as some conservative complementarians might see it, egalitarians are doing something much more reasonable, namely employing the accepted approach of allowing numerous clear passages to serve as the grid for interpreting a more complex passage like 1 Timothy 2:9–15. And given the number of unqualified Pauline passages on gifts, the numbers are in egalitarians' favor for doing so, especially since 1 Timothy 2:9–15 originally would have been *unknown* to churches outside of Ephesus. In fact, egalitarians are taking to heart one of Blomberg's important reminders:

> We ... remind interpreters again that much depends on the theological grids they presuppose when they approach a text. ... [This] is acute for the Epistles of Paul, since nowhere else in Scripture do so many different documents come from the same writer. If a minor point in one document develops into a major point for all, or vice-versa, interpretation will be skewed.[26]

What egalitarians seek, therefore, is not a "skewed" perspective but rather a balanced one that doesn't allow 1 Timothy 2:9–15 to color all of Paul's other passages that address gifts.

Truth and Consequences

Now if conservative complementarians are correct, then "no harm, no foul," as the saying goes. In other words, their hermeneutical approach hurts no one. But if conservative complementarians are wrong, then women in complementarian local churches will spend their entire lives with their gifts significantly underutilized. And while there may be nothing overtly immoral about this, since the women are restricting the use of their gifts in submission to the theology imposed by the male church leaders, it doesn't change the fact that God's resources will not be deployed as they ought to be. For example, rather than five talents producing five more talents, we may only see the five talents produce one, because gifted female teachers and pastors were significantly limited in their activities. Stated differently, if life is primarily a training ground for all that will come in the eternal kingdom of God,[27] then to directly prevent women from developing and using their gifts, or failing to encourage them in doing so, is to leave them weakened in this life and less prepared for the eternity to come. Again, conservative complementarians could be right, but this is not at all certain, and the consequences—both to women and the church as a whole—of an incorrect or overly restrictive interpretive grid could be severe.

Consider another example. One of the sermon illustrations that Pastor Timothy Keller has repeatedly used was given to him by a female Bible teacher.[28] Although it was spoken many years before, Keller has remarked how this illustration still contributes to his own teaching and view of God. (This is an amazing comment, because Keller co-founded The Gospel Coalition *with John Piper*.) I'm just one of many who have been greatly blessed by Keller over the years, and the church would be all the poorer if Keller had never benefitted from the opportunity to learn from this godly female teacher. If church leaders continue to discourage women from speaking and teaching men in any formal capacity, then we can only guess how many limbs they are amputating off the body of Christ.

The parables of the talents and minas, along with the uncertainty surrounding the proper interpretation of 1 Timothy 2:9–15, suggest that the wisest and likely the most biblically faithful course would be to encourage the exercise of women's gifts, including the important gift of teaching, as universally as possible, and only impose limitations when Scripture *unequivocally* (or unmistakably) mandates that doing so is necessary. For example, even if the leaders of your faith community see within Scripture a coherent interpretation that limits teaching roles to men alone, this still doesn't excuse wasting the gifts of women in the church. Regarding the gift of prophecy, Blomberg writes that "One should, in fact, phrase things more strongly: not to encourage a woman who appears to have the gift of prophecy to cultivate it in the context of preaching God's word to his people is to fight against God's spiritual gifts to all his followers—especially for the edification of the entire body (Eph. 4:13)."[29]

The same logic would seem to apply to the gift of teaching. But when individuals in positions of spiritual authority over a body of believers elevate the somewhat speculative theology of "biblical manhood and womanhood" to a place of higher importance over the use of spiritual gifts, damage can be done in the very name of "biblical fidelity." I use the term "speculative" because, as egalitarians have noted, there is really very little spoken directly about, or solely with regard to, women in Scripture. For example, as Westfall points out, historically many of the verses that mention men have been ascribed to men alone, even though contextually these verses apply to all believers, and those few that speak to women alone are isolated.[30] "The prayer of a righteous man is powerful and effective" is how the 1984 edition of my NIV Study Bible renders James 5:16, but the 2011 version now renders "man" as "person" to reflect the fact that the prayers of righteous women may also be powerful and effective. This is in no way to argue for a removal of gendered language from Scripture. Rather, I want to highlight that in many instances the term "man" has traditionally been selected by translators even though the term "person" would work just as well because the verse applies to believers of both genders. The parable of the talents is no exception:

> As in the story of the talents in Matthew 25:14–28, women are under a sacred obligation to use all of what God has given them and every advantage to serve him. Women must resist any effort to squeeze their strengths, gifts, and abilities into a mold that hides them in the ground and quenches the Holy Spirit.[31]

Again, the failure to use the gifts that you have received from God appears to be much more than just slothful behavior. Based on the ending to the parable, it would seem to be immoral as well. Since women face this sacred obligation as much as men, any prohibitions on the use of spiritual gifts within the body of Christ based on gender, rather than fitness or qualification, should only be implemented with the utmost care, and really only to the extent absolutely necessary.[32] If these prohibitions are somehow furthering the burying of female talents into the proverbial ground, then those who overly or wrongly limit women's gifts are *morally* complicit in their dereliction.[33]

The argument against greater inclusion of women is even sometimes based on the inherent differences that supposedly make men universally better teachers and leaders. As we saw in chapter 6, this argument is based upon the assumption that men are more inclined toward "rational analysis" and women are more "susceptible to deception." Even complementarians like Schreiner have come to realize the disturbing implications of such a theory: "[I]t seems that this view also strays from the text, even if one agrees that such differences exist between men and women. If Paul argued that women were deceived because of innate dispositions, the goodness of God's creative work is called into question."[34] Rather, it's precisely because of our differences that both genders are needed as full participants in the work of the body of Christ.

Unity in Diversity

Despite egalitarians' ringing endorsement of Paul's statement "nor is there male and female, for you are all one in Christ Jesus" (Gal. 3:28), they *do* recognize the obvious truth that men and women are different (physiologically, psychologically, and biochemically), and that they possess different strengths and weaknesses. But rather than stifle or limit the exercise of women's gifts in the church, egalitarians embrace their own form of complementary theology which recognizes that the church's strength comes in part from the wonderful unity in diversity that we can experience because of the redemptive work of Christ. The different strengths of men and women are complementary, and therefore to relegate approximately one-half of the persons (i.e., the women) in a congregation or faith community to the ministry sidelines is to indelibly weaken it.

I have one final illustration. In 2005, historian Doris Kearns Goodwin published a fascinating account of the presidency of Abraham Lincoln entitled *A Team of Rivals*. Her in-depth work tracks Lincoln's counterintuitive but brilliant decision to select the members of his Cabinet (i.e., the heads of the executive departments) from among the very men who competed against him for the presidency. Working with such rivals, many of whom held different views from Lincoln, was no doubt quite exhausting at times. However, it provided Lincoln with contrary viewpoints that added balance and sharpened his own ideas. Even in more modern times, jurists like the late Justice Antonin Scalia of the U.S. Supreme Court have employed a "counter-clerk," meaning someone who would usually read the law with an entirely opposing viewpoint to his own, in addition to his like-minded clerks. The church can learn a valuable lesson from such examples. Or rather, it can reclaim a lesson that it seems to have forgotten. The differing personalities, observations, perspectives, and gifts of men and women have much to offer the church, for both are needed and are part of God's design, and those in positions of teaching and spiritual authority may be hurting the churches they lead by limiting or restricting the gifts of women without a clear mandate to do so.

Building a Better Theology of Gifts

It appears inconsistent to ignore the lessons of the parables of the talents and minas, the lengthy gift discussion in Romans

12, and every other unqualified exhortation in the New Testament to use and cultivate your gifts and resources—regardless of gender—for the glory of God, simply because of seven verses that Paul wrote to Timothy.[35] The passages in 1 Peter 4:10-11, James 2:14-26, and 1 John 3:16-18 were not even written by Paul, so it makes no sense to interpret them with 1 Timothy 2:9-15 in mind. Moreover, even within Paul's letters to other churches, such as the gift passages in Romans 12:1-8 and 1 Corinthians 12:1-11, Paul makes no mention of the prohibitions in 1 Timothy 2:12-14. Therefore, the original recipients of these letters in Rome and Corinth, respectively, would also have had no reason to interpret them with 1 Timothy 2:9-15 in mind, since Paul's letter to Timothy was sent to Ephesus. Only years later, as the Pauline corpus was assembled,[36] would a comparison between 1 Timothy 2:9-15 and Paul's other letters have even been possible. If one of the general rules of hermeneutics is that we "must determine the impact that the biblical message would have had in its original setting," so that interpreters "should seek to know . . . how the original recipients would have reacted to what was written,"[37] then there is little reason to think that 1 Timothy 2:9-15 would have had an initial impact on any church other than the one in Ephesus.

If that is the case, since Paul wrote 1 Timothy as well as the letters to Rome and Corinth, we're forced to conclude that Paul was either a very mercurial writer or else he was revealing principles *in each letter* that transcend time, culture, and hairstyles. The latter conclusion seems preferable given the doctrines of biblical inerrancy and inspiration (2 Tim. 3:16). But if Romans 12:1-8 and 1 Corinthians 12:1-11 also teach transcultural principles, then it certainly cannot be "going beyond what is written" (1 Cor. 4:6) to administer spiritual gifting tests to women, to encourage women in the full use of their gifts, and to actively seek to develop women's gifts and their application in the body of Christ. Sadly though, this isn't what women in many churches experience, as I learned firsthand when trying to plan the women's retreat.

While the old rabbinical view that it's "better to burn the words of the Torah than to give it to women"[38] may have fallen out of favor, an alternative and crasser version of such sentiments once reached these female ears at a Protestant church: "Teaching a woman is like peeing into the wind." I'm not sure why a lavatory was unavailable to this particular gentleman, but perhaps we can attribute the comment to some mental lapse induced by dehydration from too much outdoor activity. Nevertheless, the implication seems to be that when women receive too much education they will want to grow into those who are "able to teach," and then male leaders have the problem of what to do with female teachers who are not content to "submit" to the views of conservative complementarians and only utilize their gifts with children or in women's Bible studies.[39] Certainly, both children and women need to be trained by gifted teachers, and these are invaluable arenas for teachers of both genders to exercise their gifts. Neither side of the debate is disputing this point. However, if women possess such gifts, why shouldn't the entire community—women *and* men—benefit from them as well? *That* is the real dispute.

Egalitarians are also apt to point out that placing limits on women in the exercise and development of their gifts, such as the gift of teaching, is contrary to the work of the Holy Spirit. Stanley Grenz writes:

> The New Testament presents a gender-inclusive conception of spiritual gifts (or *charismata*). Paul indicates that lying behind all gifts, regardless of who receives them, is

a common source—God (1 Cor 12:6, 28). Gifts are given not on the basis of human merit but by the will of the sovereign Holy Spirit (1 Cor 12:7-11) and the risen Christ (Eph 4:7, 11). The Spirit's endowments are bestowed on each believer, not merely a select few. The Lord of the church accords these gifts for the good of the church as a whole (1 Cor 12:7) and the completion of the common task of Christ's people (Eph 4:12).[40]

There is no reason to think that the *distribution* of gifts is limited based on gender. I believe even the most conservative complementarians would agree with this statement; their concern is with the *use* of gifts, not how the Spirit distributes them. But they may also wonder why metaphors such as "keeping women on the ministry sidelines" or "amputating part of the body of Christ" are being bandied about if women are free to exercise their gifts of teaching with children and other women. After all, it's not as if women are denied access to all avenues of ministry.

It's certainly true that women can utilize their teaching gifts with children and other women. I'm personally indebted to many godly women who have taught and invested time in me and my children, but the complementarian system (in which I served for years) now looks upon gift development in women with suspicion and as a possible challenge to biblical orthodoxy. Moreover, when male leaders teach from the pulpit, book, or blog (or all three) that the biblical, God-honoring model for the church doesn't allow for women to teach men in any biblical capacity,[41] this creates a *structural* limitation to the development of women's gifts.

For example, suppose a woman possesses the gift of teaching—imparted by the Holy Spirit—and she chooses to attend a conservative, complementarian seminary because the school is highly rated and she aligns with its "distinctives" in all other theological facets. Because of her gender and the school's theological position, she may not be permitted to exercise or develop her gifts as much as men during her training, such as in her homiletics class where preaching skills are cultivated but male students are present. How can a teacher with a God-given gift be further developed when she isn't permitted to practice her craft? Can a co-pilot ever fly a plane without logging hundreds of hours of flight time? The gift of teaching must be honed and cultivated for growth and active service. If this weren't so, then why has a single brick ever been laid at any seminary here or abroad? Gifts are a wonderful starting point for those who possess them and desire to use them for God's glory, but without stewardship, mentorship, and ceaseless encouragement they can so easily molder away. Even Paul recognized this: "Don't let anyone look down on you because you are young, but set an example for the believers in speech, in conduct, in love, in faith and in purity.... Do not neglect your gift, which was given you through prophecy when the body of elders laid their hands on you" (1 Tim. 4:12, 14).

This ceaseless encouragement is particularly needed *from* those who possess power in our faith communities *by* those who lack it, namely ethnic minorities, the economically disadvantaged, and women. As Michelle Lee-Barnewall observes:

> The Spirit is God's empowerment, and he is given to all believers. This gifting may result in "equality," although in the context of God's purposes it is better understood as leading to "inclusion," since the dominant concern is not the individual rights and benefits but God's grace to all his people, Jew and gentile, male and female.... The focal point is not the believers but God, who is preparing

a people for himself and to make himself known to the nations.[42]

If the focus of gifts is "not the believers but God," for the purpose of equipping the saints for action in proclaiming the gospel to the nations, then "inclusion" rather than "exclusion" seems the better supported biblical principle. Os Guinness echoes this point:

> In the biblical understanding of giftedness, gifts are never really ours or for ourselves. We have nothing that was not given us. Our gifts are ultimately God's, and we are only "stewards"—responsible for the prudent management of property that is not our own. This is why our gifts are always "ours for others," whether in the community of Christ or the broader society outside, especially the neighbor in need.[43]

Consequently, it's by no means greed, pride, or usurpation for a woman to insist upon being able to fully exercise her gifts without restriction. Rather, it's fundamentally an issue of faithful biblical stewardship, one that is motivated by an earnest desire to heed Paul's words: "Therefore, as we have opportunity, let us do good to all people, especially to those who belong to the family of believers" (Gal. 6:10). This point is too well attested by numerous unambiguous passages of Scripture to be undermined by conservative complementarians' narrow reading of 1 Timothy 2:9–15.

Conclusion

Tying these many biblical threads together, we can finally distill the major themes and principles that support women developing, cultivating, and exercising *all* of their God-given gifts:

1. Gifts are apportioned by the Holy Spirit and Jesus (1 Corinthians 12:1–11; Ephesians 4:11–13).

2. Teaching is one of the more significant gifts given by Jesus and the Holy Spirit (Romans 12:3–8; 1 Corinthians 12:1–11; Ephesians 4:11–13). Moreover, women are eligible to receive the gift of teaching (Joel 2:28–29).

3. The exercise of our gifts for God's glory is a universal and everlasting moral command in Scripture, as seen for example in the parables of the talents and minas (Matthew 25:14–30; Luke 19:11–27; Romans 12:3–8; 1 Peter 4:10–11). Thus, any current limitations on the exercise of women's gifts should be imposed only with great caution and as necessitated by unequivocal passages of Scripture (1 Corinthians 4:6).

4. The prohibitions against women teaching in 1 Timothy 2:12–14 are plausibly temporary restrictions imposed by Paul due to the specific circumstances facing the church leaders in Ephesus at the time of Paul's letter.[44]

5. Consequently, a woman should be permitted to teach if circumstances reveal that the Holy Spirit has endowed her with the gift of teaching (Romans 12:3–8; 1 Corinthians 14:26b).

According to these principles, we can reasonably conclude that we are accountable to God *and* to each other for knowing, using, and developing our spiritual gifts. Gifts are only useful, though, if they are perpetually combined with a growing relationship with God through Jesus Christ in the power of the Holy Spirit. Therefore, let's not be guilty of burying the gifts we have received from God, but let's trust the divine Gift-giver to redeem our time with worthwhile pursuits, just as he redeemed our lives on the cross. If "we are God's handiwork, created in Christ Jesus to do good works, which God prepared in advance for us to do" (Eph. 2:10), then we should "work at it with all [our] heart[s], as working for the Lord" (Col. 3:23). "Let there be sung *Non nobis* and *Te Deum*."[45] To God be the glory both now and forever (2 Pet. 3:18).

CHAPTER 9
A Hidden Life: Principles for Faithful and Fruitful Action

> But the effect of her being on those around her was incalculably diffusive: for the growing good of the world is partly dependent on unhistoric acts; and that things are not so ill with you and me as they might have been, is half owing to the number who lived faithfully a hidden life, and rest in unvisited tombs.
>
> —George Eliot, *Middlemarch*

IN GEORGE ELIOT's fictional work *Middlemarch*, the heroine Dorothea is a beautiful example of one who possesses the gifts of serving and showing mercy to others. Although Dorothea's gifts are far different from the ones that she had always hoped to possess, she nevertheless uses her resources and abilities to the fullest extent possible. As a result, the entire community of Middlemarch is enriched by her selfless decision to use the means at her disposal for the benefit of others. In this fictional setting, Dorothea went and served others as a true neighbor would.

Scripture is clear that we have all received gifts from the Holy Spirit who apportions them as he chooses (1 Cor. 12:11). Many of us are probably like Dorothea in some ways, possessing certain gifts and means when we would prefer others instead. And like Dorothea, we face a critical question: Will we accept and use our gifts to serve others, or will we instead lament what we don't have or cannot do? Eliot writes that "the growing good of the world is partly dependent on unhistoric acts," but this seems to be true of the kingdom of God as well. Christians are encouraged to give and pray in secret (Matt. 6:1–6); ours is a faith that encourages heroic anonymity. There will no doubt be many in heaven "who lived faithfully a hidden life" in this world but will hear "Well done, good and faithful servant!" (Matt. 25:21) in the eternity to come. Keeping score is difficult in this world, but in heaven we are assured that "the sower and the reaper [will] be glad together" (John 4:36).

A Life of Worship

After making the best decision that can be made in this earthly life—turning from sin and accepting the hope of forgiveness and eternal life that we have through Jesus Christ—a whole new world unfolds before you. Immediately you gain an enormous new family of brothers and sisters, mentors and friends, a new community that is built on the foundation of the gospel.

In *The Weight of Glory*, C. S. Lewis writes that we "are half-hearted creatures, fooling about with drink and sex and ambition when infinite joy is offered us, like an ignorant child who wants to go on making mud pies in a slum because he cannot imagine what is meant by the offer of a holiday at the sea. We are far too easily pleased."[1] In many ways, the decision to trust in Christ is a decision to say "No" to the unsatisfying mud pies of the world and "Yes" to the satisfying things that God has to offer (Ps. 16:11). This is all a wonderful and joyous change to the limited scope of life before Christ. To delve deeper into community, new believers are almost universally encouraged to join a local church where they can expand their faith, serve, grow, and learn more about this great Savior that we love. To quote Lewis once more, again with one of his insightful visual metaphors, "each one of us has got to enter that pattern, [and] take his place in that dance"[2] that is God's grand story. To say it another way using a common sports phrase, we need to "get in the game."

The famed archbishop William Temple defined "worship" as follows: "Worship is the submission of all of our nature to God. It is the quickening of the conscience by his holiness; the nourishment of mind with his truth; the purifying of imagination by his beauty; the opening of the heart to his love; the surrender of will to his purpose—all this gathered up in adoration, is the most selfless emotion of which our nature is capable."[3] Paul makes the same point in more concise terms, explaining that our entire lives should be one grand spiritual act of worship (Rom. 12:1–2).

If this is so, how then can we live out this dance without devoting the very best gifts that we have, and encouraging those we see in others, all to the glory of God? If we don't know or don't use the gifts that we possess as part of this dance, then we must in some ways be limiting ourselves (and others) to only tapping a foot as we stand at the edge of the celebration. The apostle Paul's analogy of the church as a body (Eph. 5:23) teaches us that there are no dispensable parts; all are needed and invaluable. God has prepared good works for us in advance (Eph. 2:10), and thus there is no time for Christian wallflowers.[4]

Pastor Timothy Keller has mentioned that one of the deep

flaws among secular worldviews, and sometimes even among Christians, is that we have a tendency to see ourselves as the lead actor in our own play.[5] We view our gifts, our resources, and our time as just that—ours. In actuality we are, if willing, participants in a much larger and grander story: a dance in which we revolve around and worship one God in three persons. There is no room in this narrative for us to use our gifts to indulge in self-absorption or the amassing of luxuries. Since we were bought at a high price, the precious blood of Jesus (1 Cor. 6:20), a life focused on comfort and ease and fundamentally on ourselves would diminish the infinite price that was paid to ransom us from sin (Mark 10:45).

Joining the Dance

Hopefully this book has encouraged you to "join the dance" and put your gifts to maximal use. However, now that we have covered the debate, the concepts of gender roles and calling, and fundamental biblical principles pertaining to gifts, you might be wondering where to go from here. The reminder of James, the half-brother of Jesus, is quite appropriate: "Do not merely listen to the word, and so deceive yourselves. Do what it says" (James 1:22). In other words, knowledge without application is wasted. Since application is essential, what comes next? How does a faithful Christian put this information into practice?

These are the same questions I wrestled with during the years that I spent researching these issues and forming my views. Because each woman's situation is unique, detailed guidelines or definite instructions are equally impractical. The *specific* steps that I took will not work for everyone. However, there are certain *general* principles that can assist any woman in determining a way forward. Principles are useful because they are broad and elastic; they can be adapted to fit different contexts and challenges. What follows is a roadmap of the principles that I utilized in my own life, precepts which I believe can assist any woman with navigating her unique circumstances. With some modifications, these principles apply equally to faithful Christian men.

Principle #1: Know and Develop Your Gifts

Make it a point to know and develop your spiritual gifts. More specifically, invest the time and energy to initially determine which gifts the Holy Spirit has given you, and then invest further time and effort into cultivating and honing the use of those gifts. A faithful steward knows the inventory—the valuable assets—entrusted to her. This in turn helps the steward to put the assets to their best possible use. Knowledge is necessary for effective deployment, and therefore this requires more than mere guesswork.

A good starting point is to look for your natural abilities and godly passions. What are you *already* good at? Moreover, what ministry activities excite you? What do you dream about? If each of us is "fearfully and wonderfully made" (Ps. 139:14), then our bents, personalities, and natural abilities are valuable data points in identifying our gifts. But this is only the beginning. I have personally found that experience in general, and failure in particular, is an excellent teacher. Especially in your younger years, serving in a variety of ministries and taking calculated risks are effective ways to sift speculation from reality. Numerous gift assessment tests have been developed, although some are admittedly better than others. A spiritual gifts test can be a useful starting point, but just like any extra-biblical test or guide, there are limitations. Most likely these tests would serve to point you in a general direction of gifting, although utilizing these tools cannot replace the important experience of attempting new pursuits. It does take a great deal of vulnerability to assess the gifts we possess and those with which we're not endowed. However, given the charge of the Great Commission and the parables of the talents and minas, it seems to be a worthy and wise use of energy.

While it's certainly true that some gifts can be developed and grown, it seems most practical to start with your natural gifts from the Lord and to not chase after the ones that you desire more. I would love to be a gifted singer and participate more formally in worship services, but since I'm unable to carry a tune without a sturdy bucket, I should likely concentrate my energies elsewhere besides voice lessons and songwriting classes. As Timothy Keller mentioned in a sermon about spiritual gifts and graces, you know the gifts you possess by the "kinds of needs you vibrate to, the kinds of work you enjoy, and the kinds of tasks that you succeed in."[6] These are the endeavors worth investigating and trying. If it turns out that you don't have a particular ability or don't excel at a particular task, then you can adapt as needed, but let's not grow weary of doing good (Gal. 6:9).

Once you feel like your gifts have been identified, begin working to develop them. If your gift is teaching, read the works of other gifted teachers, listen to their presentations or sermons, and study their methods. For example, in his free time, my husband is active as a Christian apologist. One summer, he invested the time and funds to spend three full days in Iowa at a "Young Communicators" conference where an older, more experienced apologist passed on a great deal of practical knowledge and wisdom to those in attendance. This is just an example. If someone in your community has cultivated their gifts or is using them in a way that you want to emulate, introduce yourself and offer to buy them lunch in return for an hour of their time. The key is to take initiative and not wait for mentors or opportunities to come to you.

I do have one caveat: A perpetual focus on your gifts and abilities can run the risk of developing narcissism or, alternatively, inertia. Self-examination should be done with humility and with God's glory in mind, not self-promotion. If your glory, fame, or self-worth enter the equation, something is sure to go wrong at some point. There can also be paralysis by analysis. Honest feedback and accountability are critical, which takes me to my next point.

Principle #2: Make Godly Friends

While you work on learning and developing your gifts, you should also make it a point to make godly friends. Rather than being a Christian lone wolf, surround yourself with loving, honest, and sincere followers of Christ who will encourage you to go further than you would naturally go on your own. Give them permission to speak truth into your life, even if you know it may hurt at times (Prov. 27:6). I see great value in being part of a local church, with its worship, ordinances, teaching and care ministries, and accountability. However, our *primary* biblical community—those with whom we share our hearts, our dreams, and our struggles and fears—may sometimes be found elsewhere. These are the people who will help you to sort out your gifts, support you when you fail, and cheer you on when you succeed.

Principle #3: Know Your Convictions

Another important principle is to know your convictions. Do your research, and understand *what* you believe and *why* you believe it. Figure out where you fall on the complementarian-egalitarian spectrum and what you can live with. This book has already mentioned a number of works that wrestle with this issue. I have included a bibliography at the end of this book that provides some additional resources for the interested reader. Accessibility is indeed an issue for many of these books (at least it was for me), which is why I took the time to pen this volume, but if you have a particular area of continued questioning then these might serve you well. As you read and study this issue in greater detail, pray and ask God for wisdom, who promises to give it abundantly to those who ask (James 1:5).

Principle #4: Put Your Gifts to Use

Once you have decided on your convictions and principles, put your gifts to use, wherever you are in life, and encourage others to do the same. This world is a training ground for eternity.[7] There is no time for sitting on the sidelines. We must labor with a kingdom perspective, rather than a temporal one.

Principle #5: Be Alert to Sexual Temptations and Tensions

As you step out and work together with brothers in Christ in various settings, you need to be mindful of the possibility of sexual temptations, and alert and sensitive to any tensions that may undermine your ministry. For women this requires that we be as wise as serpents and as innocent as doves (Matt. 10:16). When you sense the weakness of someone in the sexual realm, you will have to find ways to lovingly skirt around it (if it's a minor offense of attraction) or firmly confront it (if it's a major offense of abuse or adultery) with the help of others. If a man is uncomfortable or says foolish things around you, it may not be for reasons of theology or sexism but for reasons of attraction, and then it will be up to you to handle yourself in a wise manner that honors both him and you as fellow human beings.

Some complementarians may claim that sexual tensions and temptations would not be so prevalent if only men were serving in church leadership, but sadly, I believe we can all come up with stories of conservative complementarian church members and leaders who have fallen from grace. No one is safe, and it's up to each of us to walk so closely with the Spirit that we don't stray.

Principle #6: Do Not Be Constrained by Others

The sixth principle is to not let others be the reason you do or do not utilize your gifts. Ultimately, you answer to God, not another human being. If you feel unappreciated or constrained by others in utilizing your gifts, respectfully raise the issue, without angrily demanding attention or your "rights." If you are ignored, rebuffed, or denied, but don't feel that it's acceptable to "move on," seek other opportunities elsewhere. Serve where you are welcomed and needed, or where you sense God has definitely placed you to serve. If the situation becomes intolerable, consider leaving as a last resort.

Principle #7: Encourage the Development of Others' Gifts

When you see gifts in others in your faith community, encourage and affirm those individuals in the full use of their gifts. Don't let a spirit of jealousy or pride prevent your ability to rejoice with those who are rejoicing (Rom. 12:15). Challenge those with gifts to develop and use them to the greatest measure possible (Heb. 10:24). Almost all of us have some degree of power in a sphere of influence. Let's not sit idly by and watch missed opportunities unfold because those who are gifted lack the power to use or develop their gifts.[8] Many gifted believers who are people of color, are economically disadvantaged, or bear the scars that the broken world and broken people have given to them don't have the same power. We as fellow brothers and sisters in Christ need to boldly encourage and act as ambassadors for those who lack power. There can be no loss and surely only gain for more people, both men and women, to grow in their knowledge of God, his Word, and the ways that they can share the gospel using the gifts that the Holy Spirit has given them.

Principle #8: Live Out Your Convictions with Humility and Graciousness

Finally, whatever your convictions, live them out with a demeanor of humility and graciousness, recognizing that this is an issue about which sincere and dedicated Christians can legitimately disagree. To hone your ability to live with differences, place yourself in some level of community with those who differ from you on this topic. This doesn't mean that you need to necessarily join an Acts 29 church if you are an egalitarian or vice versa, but a diverse theological community cultivates a unifying love which is integral to working out the gospel in our broken world. A common goal of reflecting the love of Jesus through acts of service can refocus our perspectives in a much needed way. As Rebecca Manly Pippert writes in *Out of the Salt Shaker and Into the World*, "The fields are indeed ripe and ready to be harvested. What God needs are laborers. . . . I've said it before, but I will say it again: God made us different."[9] In this context, Pippert is speaking about the different ways that we, as unique individuals, can share the gospel with those around us, but the same would hold true for all God-given gifts. We are all made in God's image, male and female, and though we are different in a number of ways, both men and women alike are necessary and indispensable.

If we truly do view each other as immortal beings made in the image of God, then there should be no need for any discussion for a demand of rights. We would be so concerned with the elevation of others and their gifts above ourselves and our pride that such conversations would never even enter our minds. If rights are being demanded, or even politely requested, within the body of Christ then we are somehow missing the mark to which Jesus called us of loving our neighbors and loving God himself. As C. S. Lewis writes in *The Weight of Glory*:

> It may be possible for each to think too much of his own potential glory hereafter; it is hardly possible for him to think too often or too deep about that of his neighbour. The load, or weight, or burden of my neighbour's glory should be laid on my back, a load so heavy that only humility can carry it, and the backs of the proud will be broken.[10]

I don't want to be guilty of wrongly attacking my conservative complementarian neighbors or of failing to treat them graciously. Not one letter herein was penned in an effort to diminish the many great things that they are doing (or have done) for the kingdom of God. Rather, I wrote this book out of a deep hope for change that will benefit one-half of their congregations, both now and in the future.

In Ephesians 2:10, Paul writes that we "are God's workmanship, created in Christ Jesus to do good works, which God prepared in advance for us to do." The Greek word translated as "workmanship" is not referring to coarse, hand-hewn tools and implements. Rather, the word is *poiēma*, from which we obtain the word "poem."[11] Paul is highlighting that each one of us is a stunningly beautiful work of art crafted by God. You display that breathtaking work of art—the poem, the song, composed by God—when you walk with the Lord Jesus and live as a uniquely gifted and indispensable part of the body of Christ. May we all redeem the days that we have graciously been given, for God's glory both now and forever. Amen.

Notes

Introduction

1. Deaconesses were around for centuries in the early church. Not only was Phoebe a deaconess (Rom. 16:1), but deaconesses are mentioned in the Didascalia Apostolorum (Teaching of the Apostles), a document from the third century, and in a letter authored by the pagan ruler Pliny the Younger in the early part of the second century. The Council of Chalcedon in A.D. 451 went so far as to lay down a few counsels for the ordination of deaconesses. However, deaconesses faded in the West in the sixth century, and later disappeared in the East in the twelfth century, due in no small part to the introduction of purity laws (i.e., menstruation) from the Old Testament into the medieval church. Kenneth J. Collins and Jerry L. Walls, *Roman but Not Catholic: What Remains at Stake 500 Years after the Reformation* (Grand Rapids, MI: Baker, 2017), 171–73.
2. The prefix "para" in "parachurch" is Greek for "beside" or "alongside." Thus, parachurch organizations are typically Christian organizations (usually organized as nonprofit entities) that carry out their mission "alongside" the local church, although often independently of church oversight.

3. The word "apologetic," as in "Christian apologetics," comes from this Greek word that means "defense." It's used by the apostle Peter in 1 Peter 3:15.

4. For example, any student of American history should be familiar with the valuable insight that Alexis de Tocqueville brought to the conversation about democracy in this nation. Though he was a French historian and not necessarily an amateur in general—he was rather more of a cultural outsider—we still study his writings more than a century later because of the profound and lasting insights that he gleaned from his journey to America. However, please don't mistake that comment as any deep comparison between the two of us. I clearly would not be fit to cook croissants in the kitchen of that gentleman's French manor house.

5. Another great example of this is the *Journal of Recreational Mathematics*, which published the findings of amateurs from 1968 until its last edition in 2014.

6. Moreover, to dismiss an argument from a non-expert source merely because it is such would be to commit an informal logical fallacy. As logicians know, an argument stands or falls on its own merits, irrespective of its source or the credentials (or lack thereof) of the person who advances it.

Chapter 1

1. While Mark Driscoll is no longer the pastor at this now defunct church, he is worth mentioning given his active involvement with other ministries such as Acts 29 and The Gospel Coalition, both of which will be referenced later in this book.

2. Mark Driscoll, "Church Needs Dudes" (video of interview with *Desiring God*, April 2006), accessed May 20, 2018, https://www.youtube.com/watch?v=lex6orNNzTs.
3. The Danvers Statement was formulated in 1987 by the Council on Biblical Manhood and Womanhood (CBMW) at a meeting held in Danvers, Massachusetts. The Danvers Statement consists of ten rationales and ten affirmations summarizing the CBMW's "core beliefs," such as the belief that "some governing and teaching roles within the church are restricted to men." The Council on Biblical Manhood and Womanhood, *The Danvers Statement on Biblical Manhood and Womanhood*, accessed February 25, 2018, http://www.grbc.net/wp-content/uploads/2015/09/The-Danvers-Statement-on-Biblical-Manhood-and-Womanhood.pdf.
4. John Piper, "A Vision of Biblical Complementarity: Manhood and Womanhood Defined According to the Bible," in *Recovering Biblical Manhood and Womanhood: A Response to Evangelical Feminism*, eds. John Piper and Wayne Grudem (Wheaton, IL: Crossway, 2006), 35.
5. Ibid., 53.
6. Rebecca Merrill Groothuis and Ronald W. Pierce, "Introduction," in *Discovering Biblical Equality: Complementarity without Hierarchy*, eds. Ronald W. Pierce and Rebecca Merrill Groothuis (Downers Grove, IL: InterVarsity, 2005), 13.
7. *Hamlet*, act 2, scene 2.
8. Returning once more to Shakespeare, one could say that I'm daring to play the dangerous game of the fool. Contrary to what the name may suggest, the "fool" in Shakespeare's plays served as the sharp-witted court entertainer with the

unique ability to speak truth to power. Because the fool had no power of his own and served at the king's pleasure, he could "tell it like it was" as long as he did so in a humorous way without being *too* offensive. While I cannot lay claim to a sharp wit, I do hope to otherwise function as a "fool" in this book.

9. This is not technically a "two views" book. For a helpful example of one, see Stanley N. Gundry and James R. Beck, eds., *Two Views on Women in Ministry*, rev. ed. (Grand Rapids, MI: Zondervan, 2005).

Chapter 2

1. "Horizon may be defined as one's 'preunderstanding.' It is how [one] view[s] things as a result of [one's] knowledge, experience, beliefs, education, cultural conditioning, preferences, presuppositions and worldview. Horizons are like sunglasses through which [one] looks." Michael R. Licona, *The Resurrection of Jesus: A New Historiographical Approach* (Downers Grove, IL: InterVarsity, 2010), 38.

2. Unless otherwise noted, all Bible quotations are from the 2011 edition of the New International Version.

3. William D. Mounce, *Basics of Biblical Greek Grammar*, 3rd ed. (Grand Rapids, MI: Zondervan, 2009), 22–54.

4. The word *exegesis* basically means "to lead out of." Fundamentally, exegesis is concerned with discovering the true meaning of the text based on its grammar, syntax, and context. The opposite of exegesis is *eisegesis*, which involves reading one's meaning into the text.

5. S. M. Baugh, "A Foreign World: Ephesus in the First Century," in *Women in the Church: An Interpretation*

and *Application of 1 Timothy 2:9-15*, eds. Andreas J. Köstenberger and Thomas R. Schreiner, 3rd ed. (Wheaton, IL: Crossway, 2016), 42-43.

6. Rebecca Merrill Groothuis, "Equal in Being, Unequal in Role: Exploring the Logic of Woman's Subordination," in *Discovering Biblical Equality: Complementarity without Hierarchy*, eds. Ronald W. Pierce and Rebecca Merrill Groothuis (Downers Grove, IL: InterVarsity, 2005), 302.

7. Michelle Lee-Barnewall, *Neither Complementarian nor Egalitarian: A Kingdom Corrective to the Evangelical Gender Debate* (Grand Rapids, MI: Baker, 2016), 28-47.

8. Walter L. Liefeld, "A Plural Ministry View: Your Sons and Daughters Shall Prophesy," in *Women in Ministry: Four Views*, eds. Bonnidell Clouse and Robert G. Clouse (Downers Grove, IL: InterVarsity, 1989), 141-42.

9. Thomas R. Schreiner, "Introduction," in Köstenberger and Schreiner, 21.

10. Piper explains the reason for his vigorous complementarian efforts as a response to (1) "the increasing prevalence and acceptance of hermeneutical oddities devised to reinterpret apparently plain meanings of Biblical texts," and (2) "the consequent threat to Biblical authority as the clarity of Scripture is jeopardized and the accessibility of its meaning to ordinary people is withdrawn into the restricted realm of technical ingenuity." John Piper and Wayne Grudem, "An Overview of Central Concerns: Questions and Answers," in *Recovering Biblical Manhood and Womanhood: A Response to Evangelical Feminism*, eds. John Piper and Wayne Grudem (Wheaton, IL: Crossway, 2006), 89.

11. Timothy Keller, "The Upside Down Kingdom (Luke 6:17-26)" (MP3 podcast), March 21, 1999, accessed January

29, 2018, https://gospelinlife.com/downloads/the-upside-down-kingdom-5106/. See also Lee-Barnewall, *Neither Complementarian nor Egalitarian*, 83–119.

12. William W. Klein, Craig L. Blomberg, and Robert L. Hubbard, Jr., *Introduction to Biblical Interpretation*, 3rd ed. (Grand Rapids, MI: Zondervan, 2017), 313.

13. This graceful approach towards a stance on women in ministry was very prevalent in the scholarship of egalitarian Craig Keener and complementarian Craig Blomberg in *Two Views on Women in Ministry*. If you would enjoy reading a more in-depth treatment of the arguments, I would highly recommend this book.

Chapter 3

1. Aristotle, *Politics*, 1254.b.10, accessed March 4, 2018, http://www.perseus.tufts.edu/hopper/text?doc=Perseus%3Atext%3A1999.01.0058%3Abook%3D1%3Asection%3D1254b.

2. Tertullian, *De Cultu Feminarum*, as quoted in Cynthia Neal Kimball, "Nature, Culture and Gender Complementarity," in *Discovering Biblical Equality: Complementarity without Hierarchy*, eds. Ronald W. Pierce and Rebecca Merrill Groothuis (Downers Grove, IL: InterVarsity, 2005), 477.

3. Augustine, *On the Trinity*, 7.7.10, as quoted in Kimball, "Nature, Culture and Gender Complementarity," in Pierce and Groothuis, 476.

4. Thomas Aquinas, *Summa Theologica*, 1.92.1, as quoted in Kimball, "Nature, Culture and Gender Complementarity," in Pierce and Groothuis, 477.

5. John Piper, "A Vision of Biblical Complementarity: Manhood and Womanhood Defined According to the

Bible," in *Recovering Biblical Manhood and Womanhood: A Response to Evangelical Feminism*, eds. John Piper and Wayne Grudem (Wheaton, IL: Crossway, 2006), 51.

6. "[I]t would be hard for me to see how a woman could be a drill sergeant . . . over men without violating their sense of manhood and her sense of womanhood. . . . If a woman's job involves a good deal of directives toward men, they will need to be non-personal in general, or men and women won't flourish in the long run in that relationship without compromising profound biblical and psychological issues. And conversely, if a woman's relationship to a man is very personal, then the way she offers guidance and influence will need to be more non-directive. And my own view is that there are some roles in society that will strain godly manhood and womanhood to the breaking point. But I leave women and men in those roles to sort that out. I have never tried to make that list." John Piper, "Should Women Be Police Officers?" *Desiring God*, episode 661, August 13, 2015, accessed March 4, 2018, https://www.desiringgod.org/interviews/should-women-be-police-officers. Despite Piper's assertion about not making lists, elsewhere he provides the following list of roles that "might stretch appropriate expressions of femininity beyond the breaking point": "[1] Prime Minister and her counselors and advisors. [2] Principal and the teachers in her school. [3] College teacher and her students. [4] Bus driver and her passengers. [5] Bookstore manager and her clerks and stock help. [6] Staff doctor and her interns. [7] Lawyer and her aides. [8] Judge and the court personnel. [9] Police officer and citizens in her precinct. [10] Legislator and her assistants. [11] T.V. newscaster and her editors. [12] Counselor and her clients." Piper, "A Vision of Biblical

Complementarity," in Piper and Grudem, 50. Piper insists that he offers this list "[w]ithout passing any judgment on the appropriateness of any of these roles." However, his comment about such roles having the potential to "stretch appropriate expressions of femininity beyond the breaking point" reveals his true thoughts on the matter. Ibid.

7. Sarah Sumner, *Men and Women in the Church: Building Consensus on Christian Leadership* (Downers Grove, IL: InterVarsity, 2003), 293.

8. Craig L. Blomberg, "Women in Ministry: A Complementarian Perspective," in Stanley N. Gundry and James R. Beck, eds., *Two Views on Women in Ministry*, rev. ed. (Grand Rapids, MI: Zondervan, 2005), 177–78.

9. "Again and again scholars have observed that the discovery of the empty tomb is, in the canonical Gospels, made by women. This, they claim, is not 'the kind of detail anyone would have thought or wished to invent.' ... This is perhaps the most popular argument for the empty tomb in recent decades. ... [I]t is precisely the testimony of women, once suspect, that for us confirms the truth of the story." Dale C. Allison Jr., *Resurrecting Jesus: The Earliest Christian Tradition and Its Interpreters* (New York: T & T Clark, 2005), 326–28.

10. There is a document, dating back to the first centuries of the early church, called The Epistle to Diognetus, which records the following in its fifth chapter: "Christians ... marry like the rest of men and beget children, but they do not abandon the babies that are born. They share a common board, but not a common bed. In the flesh as they are, they do not live according to the flesh. They obey the laws

that men make, but their lives are better than the laws. They love all men, but are persecuted by all. . . . They are paupers, but they make many rich." Robert D. Culver, *Civil Government: A Biblical View* (Eugene, OR: Wipf and Stock, 2000), 272, citing *The Fathers of the Church: A New Translation* (Washington: Catholic University of America, 1962), 1:260–62.

11. Bruce L. Shelley, *Church History in Plain Language*, 2nd ed. (Nashville: Thomas Nelson, 1995), 96.

   Not long after Constantine, in A.D. 380, the emperor Theodosius made belief in Christianity a matter of imperial command. Ibid.

12. Kenneth J. Collins and Jerry L. Walls, *Roman but Not Catholic: What Remains at Stake 500 Years after the Reformation* (Grand Rapids, MI: Baker, 2017), 173.

13. Piper, "A Vision of Biblical Complementarity," in Piper and Grudem, 50–52.

14. Sumner, *Men and Women in the Church*, 89–91.

15. Jerry Bridges, *Respectable Sins* (Colorado Springs: NavPress, 2007), chapter 11.

16. I fully admit that complementarians could very well be correct in their understanding of Scripture. But even complementarians like Blomberg recognize they might also be wrong: "It is important for me to end by saying again, 'I could be wrong.' . . . If I am wrong, then I suspect the cautious (or centrist) egalitarian is correct." Blomberg, "Women in Ministry," in Gundry and Beck, 183.

   Some complementarians could learn a needed lesson about intellectual humility from their fellow complementarian. To quote Blomberg once more: "It is possible to be fully egalitarian and evangelical while maintaining

Pauline authorship [of 1 Timothy], by arguing that there are historical or textual reasons for seeing 1 Tim 2:12 as situation specific in its original intention." William W. Klein, Craig L. Blomberg, and Robert L. Hubbard, Jr., *Introduction to Biblical Interpretation*, 3rd ed. (Grand Rapids, MI: Zondervan, 2017), 544n95.

17. C. S. Lewis, "Mere Christianity," in *The Complete C. S. Lewis Signature Classics* (New York: HarperCollins, 2002), 69.

18. William Lane Craig, "Why Don't I Quote More Women Philosophers or Theologians?" *Reasonable Faith* Q&A #377, July 6, 2014, accessed February 25, 2018, https://www.reasonablefaith.org/writings/question-answer/why-dont-i-quote-more-women-philosophers-or-theologians.

19. Some might say that I'm acting in a proud manner by even writing this book and challenging the intentions of godly teachers who are more educated than I am. In response, I have sincerely tried to be fair in my analysis and criticism, calling out only flagrant comments or fallacious reasoning. The Berean Jews were praised because they compared the message of the apostle Paul against Scripture in order to test Paul's words (Acts 17:11). It has been my similar intent to compare the message of conservative complementarians against Scripture, and to note where that message seems lacking.

20. As a young girl, I even endured being called "Chet Morton" (the freckled pie-eating friend from *The Hardy Boys*) by my two brothers. Surely, indignity knows no limits among siblings.

21. Cynthia Long Westfall, *Paul and Gender: Reclaiming the Apostle's Vision for Men and Women in Christ* (Grand Rapids, MI: Baker, 2016), 216–18.

Chapter 4

1. "What We Believe," Acts 29, accessed January 21, 2018, http://www.acts29.com/about.
2. My husband was formerly an elder at a church that belonged to the Acts 29 network, and he was easily able to confirm for me that this understanding is accurate.
3. A pastor by the name of Matt Chandler is the new leader of the Acts 29 network, and in a recent interview regarding the origins of the group he described himself as follows: "It was an invitation to help build a world for those serious about theology but not crusty about it. That might sound harsh today, but 12 years ago I certainly couldn't find that world. I was Reformed in soteriology, and I was complementarian, but I also believed in the gifts of the Spirit." Sarah E. Zylstra, "How Acts 29 Survived—and Thrived—After the Collapse of Mars Hill," *The Gospel Coalition*, December 5, 2017, accessed February 25, 2018, https://www.thegospelcoalition.org/article/how-acts-29-survived-and-thrived-after-the-collapse-of-mars-hill/.

   I admit that Chandler made these comments in the context of a brief interview regarding the history of the Acts 29 network and not as part of an extensive theological discussion. Even so, it's telling that when briefly describing his theology he only mentioned three things and, whether intentionally or not, included complementarianism as one of them. One has to wonder if he would regard those who are not complementarian as "unserious about theology." It's also interesting to note the tension between his last two comments: "I was complementarian, but I also believed in the gifts of the Spirit." In many ways, the degree to which Chandler implements complementarianism as a lead pastor will determine just how limited the female members of his church will be when seeking to utilize their spiritual gifts.

4. As Christian philosopher William Lane Craig explains, "We can think of our theology like a web, with certain beliefs near the center of the web and others further out nearer the perimeter.... At the center of our web of beliefs should be certain essential doctrines like the existence of God and the deity of Christ and then a little further out the doctrine of, say, the atonement, and further out still doctrines like the sacraments and biblical inspiration and its possible corollary biblical inerrancy. If one of the central doctrines is abandoned, then the whole web, indeed, collapses. But if a belief near the circumference is discarded, while that will cause readjustments elsewhere in the web, it won't compromise the structure of the whole." William Lane Craig, "Qualms about the Resurrection of Jesus," *Reasonable Faith* Q&A #69, August 11, 2008, accessed February 25, 2018, https://www.reasonablefaith.org/writings/question-answer/qualms-about-the-resurrection-of-jesus.

Complementarianism seems like a "further out" doctrine rather than an "essential doctrine." It should be located toward the outside of the web, not at or near the center.

5. Albert Mohler, "The Wrath of God Poured Out – The Humiliation of the Southern Baptist Convention," *Albert Mohler* (commentary), May 23, 2018, accessed June 4, 2018, https://albertmohler.com/2018/05/23/wrath-god-poured-humiliation-southern-baptist-convention/?mc_cid=45b3897781&mc_eid=c68ec614b1.

6. "Preface (2006)," in *Recovering Biblical Manhood and Womanhood: A Response to Evangelical Feminism*, eds. John Piper and Wayne Grudem (Wheaton, IL: Crossway, 2006), xii.

7. For this reason, Keener is allocated *three* chapters in Lee Strobel's new book on miracles. Lee Strobel, *The Case for Miracles: A Journalist Investigates Evidence for the Supernatural* (Grand Rapids, MI: Zondervan, 2018), 73–117.

8. Ligon Duncan, Chancellor, Reformed Theological Seminary, endorsement of John Piper and Wayne Grudem, *50 Crucial Questions: An Overview of Central Concerns about Manhood and Womanhood* (Wheaton, IL: Crossway, 2016), accessed February 25, 2018, https://www.desiringgod.org/books/50-crucial-questions-about-manhood-and-womanhood.

   A similar claim is made in the preface of Piper and Grudem's other book: "At the core of this topic lies the fundamental issue of biblical authority. If we write off, ignore, or distort the Bible's teaching on gender roles, then we are bound to do so with everything the Bible teaches. . . . If we deny biblical teaching about manhood and womanhood, the possibility of a definitive interpretation is lost. If we can wrest egalitarianism from the Bible, we can pervert it to say anything we wish. Pagan ideas underlie evangelical feminism, based, as it is, on ideas borrowed from cultural feminism. Egalitarianism must always lead to an eventual denial of the gospel." "Preface (2006)," in Piper and Grudem, xi–xii.

9. After all, we're not dealing with Sabellianism, which denies the tri-personality of God, or Docetism, which denies that Jesus had a real physical body. We have enough heresies already, so let's not needlessly add to the pile.

10. "The Westminster Confession of Faith," Center for Reformed Theology and Apologetics, accessed February 25, 2018, http://www.reformed.org/documents/wcf_with_proofs/.

Chapter 5

1. William W. Klein, Craig L. Blomberg, and Robert L. Hubbard, Jr., *Introduction to Biblical Interpretation*, 3rd ed. (Grand Rapids, MI: Zondervan, 2017), 42–43.
2. Sarah Sumner, *Men and Women in the Church: Building Consensus on Christians Leadership* (Downers Grove, IL: InterVarsity, 2003), 210.
3. Thomas R. Schreiner, "A Response to Linda Belleville," in Stanley N. Gundry and James R. Beck, eds., *Two Views on Women in Ministry*, rev. ed. (Grand Rapids, MI: Zondervan, 2005), 105.
4. D. A. Carson and Douglas J. Moo, *An Introduction to the New Testament*, 2nd ed. (Grand Rapids, MI: Zondervan, 2005), 117.
5. "Interpreting Scripture with Scripture . . . or adopting what the ancients called the 'rule of faith' (*regula fide*) is always legitimate when the additional passage being used to interpret a given text would have been known to the text's author." Craig L. Blomberg with Jennifer Foutz Markley, *A Handbook of New Testament Exegesis* (Grand Rapids, MI: Baker, 2010), 230.
6. Craig S. Keener, *Paul, Women and Wives: Marriage and Women's Ministry in the Letters of Paul* (Peabody, MA: Hendrickson, 1992), xvi.
7. Thomas R. Schreiner, "Head Coverings, Prophecies and the Trinity," in *Recovering Biblical Manhood and Womanhood: A Response to Evangelical Feminism*, eds. John Piper and Wayne Grudem (Wheaton, IL: Crossway, 2006), 138.
8. Thomas R. Schreiner, *Interpreting the Pauline Epistles* (Grand Rapids, MI: Baker, 2011), 97.

9. As the *Catechism* declares, "Mindful of Christ's words to his apostles, 'He who hears you, hears me' [Luke 10:16], the faithful receive with docility the teachings and directives that their pastors give them in different forms." *Catechism of the Catholic Church*, 2nd ed. (Washington, D.C.: United States Catholic Conference, 1997), par. 87.

10. Cynthia Long Westfall, *Paul and Gender: Reclaiming the Apostle's Vision for Men and Women in Christ* (Grand Rapids, MI: Baker, 2016), 208.

11. Carson and Moo, *Introduction to the New Testament*, 465–68.

12. Gordon D. Fee, "Male and Female in the New Creation," in *Discovering Biblical Equality: Complementarity without Hierarchy*, eds. Ronald W. Pierce and Rebecca Merrill Groothuis (Downers Grove, IL: InterVarsity, 2005), 185.

13. A full defense for this verse as the proper starting point for women in ministry can be found in the egalitarian works listed in the "Further Reading" section at the end of this book. Because this defense is outside the scope of this work, I have omitted it for the sake of brevity.

14. Due to space considerations, a more in-depth discussion of Genesis 1—3, 1 Corinthians 14, and Galatians 3 is available on my website.

15. Schreiner, "Head Coverings, Prophecies and the Trinity," in Piper and Grudem, 136.

16. "Paul is not denying that women are created in God's image, for he is referring to the creation accounts here and was well aware that Genesis teaches that both women and men are created in God's image." Ibid., 132–33.

17. To be fair, the Netherlands Reformed Church and its offshoot, the Heritage Reformed Church (with which Puritan Reformed Theological Seminary in Grand Rapids is associated), do handle this matter consistently. That is, the women of these two denominations are expected to keep their heads covered in accordance with 1 Corinthians 11. But this is very much the exception among churches, not the rule.

18. Craig S. Keener, "Women in Ministry: Another Egalitarian Perspective," in Gundry and Beck, 240.

19. Ibid.

20. Thomas R. Schreiner, "Review of *Two Views on Women in Ministry*," *Journal for Biblical Manhood and Womanhood* (Fall 2001): 25–26.

21. However, Schreiner's rebuttal seems inadequate, and not only because he himself uses rhetoric to counter the "rhetorically effective" approach utilized by egalitarians. Christian apologist Greg Koukl calls this technique "narrating the debate." This involves "step[ping] outside of the conversation . . . and describ[ing] . . . the turn the discussion has taken." Gregory Koukl, *Tactics: A Game Plan for Discussing Your Christian Convictions* (Grand Rapids, MI: Zondervan, 2009), 87.

In effect, Schreiner attempts to reduce the rhetorical effectiveness of the egalitarian argument by calling attention to the fact that egalitarians are employing rhetoric to make their case. Never mind that Schreiner is using his own rhetorical device to advance his complementarian counterargument.

22. Schreiner, "Review of *Two Views on Women in Ministry*," 27.

23. Schreiner, "Head Coverings, Prophecies and the Trinity," in Piper and Grudem, 125.
24. Schreiner objects that "No egalitarian has successfully explained how an argument from the created order can be culturally relative." However, no argument has ever really been necessary in the first place. While there are, of course, traditions and cultures that do embrace head coverings as normative, the instances of church evictions related to head coverings appear to be very few indeed. Despite the fact that head coverings are very clearly tied to the created order, they don't seem to find their way onto lists of church "distinctives" and "core values" in the same way that complementarianism does.
25. As Koukl also notes, "When a cherished view is at stake, it's not unusual for people to raise empty objections—objections that initially sound worthwhile, but simply can't be defended once examined." Koukl, *Tactics*, 87.
26. Westfall, *Paul and Gender*, 33-34.
27. Schreiner, "Review of *Two Views on Women in Ministry*," 25-26.
28. Keener, "Another Egalitarian Perspective," in Gundry and Beck, 227.
29. Perhaps as an ode to their conclusion that men shouldn't be taught by women, only male contributors participate in the scholarship section of *Women in the Church*, whereas women contribute in the virtual roundtable section. Nevertheless, this volume does stand as an interesting counter-perspective to the collection of more centrist complementarian and egalitarian authorship on 1 Timothy 2:9-15.

30. Clinton Arnold and Robert Saucy, "The Ephesian Background of Paul's Teaching on Women's Ministry," in *Women and Men in Ministry: A Complementary Perspective* (Chicago: Moody, 2001), 281–83.
31. S. M. Baugh, "A Foreign World: Ephesus in the First Century," in *Women in the Church: An Interpretation and Application of 1 Timothy 2:9–15*, eds. Andreas J. Köstenberger and Thomas R. Schreiner, 3rd ed. (Wheaton, IL: Crossway, 2016), 59.
32. Westfall, *Paul and Gender*, 18–19.
33. *Oxyrhynchus papyrus* 744. G, as quoted in Mary R. Lefkowitz and Maureen B. Fant, *Women's Life in Greece and Rome: A Source Book in Translation*, 3rd ed. (Baltimore, MD: John Hopkins University Press, 2005), 187.
34. Craig S. Keener, "Learning in the Assemblies," in Pierce and Groothuis, 165.
35. Ibid., 171 (emphasis mine).
36. As others have pointed out, it's possible that Priscilla herself may have been present in Ephesus near or about this time when Paul sent his letter to Timothy. Did Priscilla violate God's commands by "explaining" the faith to Apollos (Acts 18:26)? Or was she given a "pass" because her husband was also present or because this took place in her home and not in a local church? Since many churches met inside homes, and Paul praises Priscilla and Aquila instead of asking Aquila to do a better job leading his wife, it seems fair to conclude that she acted in accordance with apostolic teaching on the matter.
37. Keener, "Another Egalitarian Perspective," in Gundry and Beck, 233.

38. Bill Mounce, *New Testament Greek Dictionary*, s.v. "ἐξουσία," accessed May 11, 2018, https://www.billmounce.com/greek-dictionary/exousia.

39. Al Wolters, "The Meaning of Αὐθεντέω," in Köstenberger and Schreiner, 65–115.

40. Linda L. Belleville, "Teaching and Usurping Authority: 1 Timothy 2:11–15," in Pierce and Groothuis, 205–23.

41. Köstenberger examines a general pattern in the New Testament involving the use of paired infinitives, a concept known as a "hendiadys." According to this pattern, because the term for "teach" is positive, the term *authenteō* must also be positive. Andreas J. Köstenberger, "A Complex Sentence: The Syntax of 1 Timothy 2:12," in Köstenberger and Schreiner, 117–61.

42. Walter L. Liefeld, "A Plural Ministry View: Your Sons and Daughters Shall Prophesy," in *Women in Ministry: Four Views*, eds. Bonnidell Clouse and Robert G. Clouse (Downers Grove, IL: InterVarsity, 1989), 127.

43. Ibid., 150.

44. Keener, *Paul, Women and Wives*, xiii.

45. Schreiner, "Review of *Two Views on Women in Ministry*," 26.

46. Thomas R. Schreiner, "Kaleidoscopic View: Penal Substitution Response," in *The Nature of the Atonement: Four Views*, eds. James Beilby and Paul R. Eddy (Downers Grove, IL: InterVarsity, 2006), 193.

47. The following comment from Blomberg is insightful: "If I am wrong, then I suspect the cautious (or centrist) egalitarian is correct. Having been immersed in the evangelical subculture since I was fifteen (in 1970), I have seen far too

many women deeply hurt by uncaring attitudes and actions or rude remarks (sometimes intended, unsuccessfully, to be humorous) by male (and occasionally female!) complementarians, normally alleged to be justifiable by their theological perspectives, for me to ever imagine adopting a more restrictive form of complementarianism than the one I now hold. On the other hand, I have only somewhat less often seen egalitarian spokespersons communicate much of anything besides an 'I demand my rights' kind of attitude. On both sides, it seems that quests for power rather than biblical obedience dominate the behavior of many." Craig L. Blomberg, "Women in Ministry: A Complementarian Perspective," in Gundry and Beck, 183.

48. Thomas R. Schreiner, "A Response to Craig Keener," in Gundry and Beck, 260.

49. Schreiner, "Review of *Two Views on Women in Ministry*," 25–26.

50. Schreiner, "A Response to Craig Keener," in Gundry and Beck, 261.

51. Justin Taylor, "A Conversation with J. D. Greear, the New President of the Southern Baptist Convention," *The Gospel Coalition*, June 12, 2018, accessed June 16, 2018, https://www.thegospelcoalition.org/blogs/justin-taylor/j-d-greear-elected-as-the-62nd-president-of-the-southern-baptist-convention/.

52. This is not merely anecdotal. As a recent Gospel Coalition article noted, "I recently spoke with some women, all of whom—eight or more years after seminary or Bible school graduation—are still seeking ministry jobs. At any given time, there are only a handful of such jobs available, and the number drops steeply in complementarian

churches (my own tradition).... Many have taken full-time work in other fields due to the lack of employment opportunities in the local church.... Many pastors have expressed to me appropriate concern that their women's ministries are reading theologically light books or only offering studies by the most popular Christian bloggers. At the same time, most pastors, due to time constraints and ministry demands, are not able to keep their ear to the ground in Christian women's circles, nor are they able to read and review every book or study sought out by the women in their congregation.... While most [pastors] said they encourage women who feel called to ministry to pursue ministry or theological training, few have women on their staff in ministry roles." Amy Gannett, "3 Reasons to Hire Women to Do Ministry in the Local Church," *The Gospel Coalition*, March 14, 2018, accessed May 14, 2018, https://www.thegospelcoalition.org/article/3-reasons-to-hire-women-to-do-ministry-in-the-local-church/.

53. I'm not suggesting here that complementarians believe female susceptibility to deception to be part of humanity's fall or an ontological component of original sin. However, that was the view of certain church fathers such as Tertullian, Augustine, and Origen.

54. "[1 Timothy 2:13–15] is crucial to understanding this passage: first because ... [it] point[s] us back to Genesis, in which God's original order was established and then disrupted by sin; second because [it] remind[s] us of God's overarching plan from the start, as [1 Timothy 2:15] concludes by echoing Genesis 3's promise of an offspring." Kathleen Nielson, *Women and God: Hard Questions, Beautiful Truth* (Denmark: The Good Book Company, 2018), 167.

55. Keener, *Paul, Women and Wives*, 117.
56. Schreiner, "A Response to Craig Keener," in Gundry and Beck, 259–60.
57. Acts 19:23–34.
58. Linda L. Belleville, "Women in Ministry: An Egalitarian Perspective," in Gundry and Beck, 89.
59. Baugh, "Ephesus in the First Century," in Köstenberger and Schreiner, 35–36.
60. Klein, Blomberg, and Hubbard, *Introduction to Biblical Interpretation*, 543.
61. Ibid.
62. Baugh, "Ephesus in the First Century," in Köstenberger and Schreiner, 42–43.
63. Nina Martin, "U.S. Has the Worst Rate of Maternal Deaths in the Developed World," *NPR*, May 10, 2017, accessed May 10, 2018, https://www.npr.org/2017/05/12/528098789/u-s-has-the-worst-rate-of-maternal-deaths-in-the-developed-world.
64. Belleville, "An Egalitarian Perspective," in Gundry and Beck, 90–91.
65. Bill Mounce, *New Testament Greek Dictionary*, s.v. "σῴζω," accessed May 11, 2018, https://www.billmounce.com/greek-dictionary/sozo.
66. Westfall, *Paul and Gender*, 137–38.
67. Thomas R. Schreiner, "An Interpretation of 1 Timothy 2:9–15: A Dialogue with Scholarship," in Köstenberger and Schreiner, 221.

Interestingly, for 1 Timothy 2:15, Schreiner seems to disregard Blomberg's hermeneutical advice: "[W]hile knowledge of the historical-cultural setting is important for discovering the intended meaning, it... must never supplant the plain meaning of the text." Klein, Blomberg, and Hubbard, *Introduction to Biblical Interpretation*, 321. And yet, Schreiner insists that egalitarians must follow this same advice when reading 1 Timothy 2:12–14, just three verses prior. This double standard is what egalitarians regard as highly questionable.

68. Sumner, *Men and Women in the Church*, 258.
69. Ibid.
70. Westfall, *Paul and Gender*, 221.

Chapter 6

1. *As You Like It*, act II, scene VII.
2. For an excellent discussion of the Bible and gender, see Abdu Murray, *Saving Truth: Finding Meaning and Clarity in a Post-Truth World* (Grand Rapids, MI: Zondervan, 2018), 117–59.
3. As some Christian theologians have noted, extending Jesus' subordination beyond the Incarnation (i.e., permanent subordination) could be problematic: "God could simply exist eternally with his multiple cognitive faculties and capacities. This is, in our view, all for the better. For although creedally affirmed, the doctrine of the generation of the Son (and the procession of the Spirit) is a relic of Logos Christology that finds virtually no warrant in the biblical text and introduces a subordinationism into the Godhead, which anyone who affirms the full deity of Christ ought to find very troubling." J. P. Moreland and William Lane Craig, *Philosophical Foundations for a Christian*

Worldview, 2nd ed. (Downers Grove, IL: InterVarsity, 2017), 593.

4. Wayne Grudem, *Systematic Theology* (Grand Rapids, MI: Zondervan, 1994), 245, 248–56.

5. Cynthia Long Westfall, *Paul and Gender: Reclaiming the Apostle's Vision for Men and Women in Christ* (Grand Rapids, MI: Baker, 2016), 4.

6. In the first version of his book published in 1995, Schreiner argued that women are more easily deceived "because of the different inclinations present in Adam and Eve. Generally speaking, women are more relational and nurturing and men are more given to rational analysis and objectivity. Women are less prone than men to see the importance of doctrinal formulations, especially when it comes to the issue of identifying heresy and making a stand for the truth. Appointing women to the teaching office is prohibited because they are less likely to draw a line on doctrinal non-negotiables, and thus deception and false teaching will more easily enter the church. This is not to say women are intellectually deficient or inferior to men. If women were intellectually inferior, Paul would not allow them to teach women and children. What concerns him are the consequences of allowing women in the authoritative teaching office, for their gentler and kinder nature inhibits them from excluding people for doctrinal error. There is the danger of stereotyping here, for obviously some women are more inclined to objectivity and are 'tougher' and less nurturing than other women. But as a general rule women are more relational and caring than men." Thomas R. Schreiner, "An Interpretation of 1 Timothy 2:9–15: A Dialogue with Scholarship," in *Women in the Church: A Fresh Analysis of 1 Timothy 2:9–15*, eds. Andreas J.

Köstenberger, Thomas R. Schreiner, and H. Scott Baldwin (Grand Rapids, MI: Baker, 1995), 145–46. It seems that Schreiner may have walked back some of these comments in the second edition of his book. Westfall, *Paul and Gender*, 115n19. However, that he ever made them at all is still somewhat shocking.

7. Grudem concludes the following from 1 Timothy 2:14: "God gave men, in general, a disposition that is better suited to teaching and governing in the church, a disposition that inclines more to rational, logical analysis of doctrine and a desire to protect the doctrinal purity of the church, and God gave women, in general, a disposition that inclines more toward a relational, nurturing emphasis that places a higher value on unity and community in the church.... Paul understands the kinder, gentler, more relational nature of women as something that made Eve less inclined to oppose the deceptive serpent and more inclined to accept his words as something helpful and true." Wayne Grudem, *Evangelical Feminism and Biblical Truth: An Analysis of More Than One Hundred Disputed Questions* (Wheaton, IL: Crossway, 2012), 72.

8. In the most general terms, "ontology" is the philosophical (or metaphysical) study of the nature of existence or being as such.

9. Raymond C. Ortlund, Jr., "Male-Female Equality and Male Headship: Genesis 1–3," in *Recovering Biblical Manhood and Womanhood: A Response to Evangelical Feminism*, eds. John Piper and Wayne Grudem (Wheaton, IL: Crossway, 2006), 111.

10. Rebecca Merrill Groothuis, "'Equal in Being, Unequal in Role': Exploring the Logic of Woman's Subordination,"

in *Discovering Biblical Equality: Complementarity without Hierarchy,* eds. Ronald W. Pierce and Rebecca Merrill Groothuis (Downers Grove, IL: InterVarsity, 2005), 304.

11. Kevin Giles, "The Subordination of Christ and the Subordination of Women," in Pierce and Groothuis, 334–52.

12. John Piper, "A Vision of Biblical Complementarity: Manhood and Womanhood Defined According to the Bible," in Piper and Grudem, 52.

13. Craig L. Blomberg, "Women in Ministry: A Complementarian Perspective," in Stanley N. Gundry and James R. Beck, eds., *Two Views on Women in Ministry,* rev. ed. (Grand Rapids, MI: Zondervan, 2005), 161.

14. Grudem, *Systematic Theology,* 776.

15. Leon Morris, *The Atonement: Its Meaning and Significance* (Downers Grove, IL: InterVarsity, 1983), 126.

16. Ibid.

17. John Piper and Wayne Grudem, "An Overview of Central Concerns: Questions and Answers," in Piper and Grudem, 76–77.

As Christian apologist Ravi Zacharias has noted, women are in fact *critical* to the work of missionaries: "Womankind in general and mothers in particular have done what the best of men could not do. There is something that combines intuition with courage that has been the incredible gift to women. Ask any missionary and they will tell you that the linguistic skills of a woman almost always exceed that of the man on the mission field. They are truly the great communicators in word and deed." Ravi Zacharias, "God's Heart Revealed in a Mother: A Mother's Day Reflection," *RZIM,* May 11, 2018, accessed May 12,

2018, https://mailchi.mp/rzim.org/gods-heart-revealed-in-a-mother?e=725fb854a6.

18. Blomberg, "A Complementarian Perspective," in Gundry and Beck, 127.

Chapter 7

1. "Sanctification" is a theological term that essentially means "growing in godliness."
2. Os Guinness, *The Call: Finding and Fulfilling The Central Purpose of Your Life* (Nashville: Thomas Nelson, 2003), 48–49.
3. Gregory Koukl, *Decision Making and the Will of God* (Stand to Reason, 2000), 28. This PDF is available from Stand to Reason and is part of the ministry's Ambassador Basic Curriculum.
4. Ibid., 29.
5. "When God speaks, He communicates specific words that are clearly understood. His revelation is objectively true, and it must be followed. *Anything less than revelation does not have authority in decision making*; it is not the pure voice of God. That does not mean that impressions in the heart should be ignored or that they cannot be helpful. . . . It just means that subjective 'voices' are not authoritative in the sense of commanding obedience." Garry Friesen, "The Wisdom View," in *How Then Should We Choose? Three Views on God's Will and Decision Making*, ed. Douglas S. Huffman (Grand Rapids, MI: Kregel, 2009), 116.
6. Koukl draws heavily from Garry Friesen, *Decision Making and the Will of God* (Portland: Multnomah, 1980).

7. John Piper, "How Do I Know God's Calling for My Life?" *Desiring God*, December 7, 2015, accessed March 12, 2018, https://www.desiringgod.org/interviews/how-do-i-know-god-s-calling-for-my-life.

8. Gordon D. Fee, "The Priority of Spirit Gifting for Church Ministry," in *Discovering Biblical Equality: Complementarity without Hierarchy*, eds. Ronald W. Pierce and Rebecca Merrill Groothuis (Downers Grove, IL: InterVarsity, 2005), 254.

9. On the one hand, Scripture tells us that "God is not human, that he should lie, not a human being, that he should change his mind" (Num. 23:19). On the other hand, we see examples of God choosing not to follow through on bringing calamity: "When God saw what they did and how they turned from their evil ways, he relented and did not bring on them the destruction he had threatened" (Jon. 3:10). So does God change his mind or not? In fact, there is no contradiction here if one accepts a Molinist view of divine foreknowledge: "Indeed, when we construe certain prophecies as counterfactual warnings, rather than as categorical declarations of simple foreknowledge, we can explain how it is that in Israel the test of a true prophet is the fulfillment of his predictions (Deut 18:22) and yet some predictions given by true prophets do not actually come to pass because the people forewarned responded in an appropriate way (Is 38:1–5; Amos 7:1–6; Jon 3:1–10). In such cases, the prophecy from God was counterfactual knowledge of what would happen under the prevailing circumstances; but were intercessory prayer or repentance to occur, then God would not carry out what had been threatened." William Lane Craig, "The Middle-Knowledge View," in *Divine Foreknowledge: Four Views*, eds. James K.

Beilby and Paul R. Eddy (Downers Grove, IL: InterVarsity, 2001), 124.

Chapter 8

1. Craig L. Blomberg, "Women in Ministry: A Complementarian Perspective," in Stanley N. Gundry and James R. Beck, eds., *Two Views on Women in Ministry*, rev. ed. (Grand Rapids, MI: Zondervan, 2005), 183.
2. Thomas R. Schreiner, *Romans* (Grand Rapids, MI: Baker, 1998), 657. Westfall offers an interesting counterpoint: "Most women in conservative churches who are gifted in the 'gray zones' that involve leadership, teaching, or other verbal gifts probably find this principle nearly impossible to follow; they fall into the practice of concentrating on ancillary roles of practical service, such as serving in the nursery and offering hospitality. It is the path of least resistance, and they are performing the actions that are most appreciated." Cynthia Long Westfall, *Paul and Gender: Reclaiming the Apostle's Vision for Men and Women in Christ* (Grand Rapids, MI: Baker, 2016), 218.
3. Douglas J. Moo, *The Epistle to the Romans* (Grand Rapids, MI: Eerdmans, 1996), 767.
4. According to its website, "Desiring God began inauspiciously in 1994 when John [Piper] handed off the church's tape ministry to his assistant, Jon Bloom." Desiring God, "About Us," accessed May 12, 2018, https://www.desiringgod.org/about-us.
5. Mary A. Kassian, "Women Teaching Men—How Far Is Too Far?" *Desiring God*, May 21, 2016, accessed May 12, 2018, https://www.desiringgod.org/articles/women-teaching-men-how-far-is-too-far.

6. She writes: "I may regard the activity as appropriate based on the following analysis: [1] Context: Non-congregational. National religious conferences are outside of the context of the local church (although denominational meetings may more closely resemble a congregational context). [2] Nature: Testimonial or inspirational. Depending on the content, the message may be more testimonial-inspirational than exegetical. [3] Authority: Non-governmental. I have no authority or responsibility for establishing standards. [4] Relationship: Impersonal. Normally there is no personal, ongoing relationship. The relationship with the listeners is quite distant, like the relationship one might have reading someone's book. As a guest speaker, I rarely even know the registrants' names. [5] Commitment: Informal. There is no formal covenant or commitment between myself and the listener, nor between him and the community. This is quite different than teaching in a Sunday service, where and when community members congregate to hear the official teaching of the church of which they are members. [6] Obligation: Voluntary. There is no obligation on the part of the listener to attend the address. It is totally discretionary and voluntary on his part (unlike the obligation of a church member to attend weekly church services and obey that teaching). [7] Constancy: Occasional. A one-time address (flying into an area, teaching, and then leaving) is very different than the ongoing corporate instruction in the context of a local church body (as it would be, say, in a Sunday school class). [8] Maturity: Mother. I have found that as I get older I have more freedom to instruct younger men as a mother instructs her son." Ibid. One would almost seem to need eight different personalities to wrestle through such a convoluted multifactor analysis.

7. Schreiner, *Romans*, 657.
8. Mimi Haddad and Alvera Mickelsen, "Helping the Church Understand Biblical Equality," in *Discovering Biblical Equality: Complementarity without Hierarchy*, eds. Ronald W. Pierce and Rebecca Merrill Groothuis (Downers Grove, IL: InterVarsity, 2005), 484.
9. As even Schreiner comments, "I believe a woman is in view. This was the majority view in the history of the church until at least the thirteenth century.... I think we can be confident Junia was a woman." Thomas R. Schreiner, "Women in Ministry: Another Complementarian Perspective," in Gundry and Beck, 286.
10. John Piper, "A Vision of Biblical Complementarity: Manhood and Womanhood Defined According to the Bible," in *Recovering Biblical Manhood and Womanhood: A Response to Evangelical Feminism*, eds. John Piper and Wayne Grudem (Wheaton, IL: Crossway, 2006), 51.
11. Judith TenElshof and Robert Saucy, "The Complementary Model of Church," in *Women and Men in Ministry: A Complementary Perspective*, eds. Judith TenElshof and Robert Saucy (Chicago: Moody, 2001), 319.
12. Blomberg, "A Complementarian Perspective," in Gundry and Beck, 152, 182.
13. Thomas R. Schreiner, "An Interpretation of 1 Timothy 2:9–15: A Dialogue with Scholarship," in *Women in the Church: An Interpretation and Application of 1 Timothy 2:9–15*, eds. Andreas J. Köstenberger and Thomas R. Schreiner, 3rd ed. (Wheaton, IL: Crossway, 2016), 222.
14. Jen Wilkin, "Women and the Church" (video of presentation, Acts 29 US Southeast Network Conference,

November 2017), accessed May 15, 2018, https://vimeo.com/243476316.

15. Shaunti and Jeff Feldhahn, *For Men Only: A Straightforward Guide to the Inner Lives of Women*, rev. ed. (Colorado Springs, CO: Multnomah, 2013), 47.

16. Judith TenElshof, "Psychological Evidence of Gender Differentiation," in TenElshof and Saucy, 235.

17. Luke 19:11–27.

18. Thomas L. Constable, *Notes on Matthew* (2017), 417, accessed May 13, 2018, http://www.soniclight.com/constable/notes/pdf/matthew.pdf.

19. Ibid., 418–19.

20. D. A. Carson, "Matthew," in *The Expositor's Bible Commentary*, vol. 8, ed. Frank E. Gaebelein (Grand Rapids, MI: Zondervan, 1984), 517.

21. Westfall, *Paul and Gender*, 217.

22. Ibid., 157, 217.

23. Piper, "A Vision of Biblical Complementarity," in Piper and Grudem, 51.

24. I'm not suggesting that eternal life or heaven are rewards for our works, for that would be contrary to Paul's teaching that salvation is through faith alone in Christ alone (Eph. 2:8–9). However, there are differing views with respect to the role that works will play when we are judged at the end of time. See *Four Views on the Role of Works at the Final Judgment*, eds. Alan P. Stanley and Stanley N. Gundry (Grand Rapids, MI: Zondervan, 2013).

25. Westfall, *Paul and Gender*, 206, 219.

26. William W. Klein, Craig L. Blomberg, and Robert L. Hubbard, Jr., *Introduction to Biblical Interpretation*, 3rd ed. (Grand Rapids, MI: Zondervan, 2017), 556–57.

27. In Luke 19:17, Jesus said those who are faithful over small things in this life will be entrusted with "cities." As Christian philosopher Dallas Willard observed, "Perhaps it would be a good exercise for each of us to ask ourselves: Really, how many cities could I now govern under God? If, for example, Baltimore or Liverpool were turned over to me, with power to do what I want with it, how would things turn out? An honest answer to this question might do much to prepare us for our eternal future in this universe." Dallas Willard, *The Divine Conspiracy* (San Francisco: HarperCollins, 1998), 398.

28. Timothy Keller, "Christ: The Final Word (Hebrews 1:1–4; 2:1–4)" (MP3 podcast), February 6, 2005, accessed May 15, 2018, https://gospelinlife.com/downloads/christ-the-final-word-5403/.

29. Blomberg, "A Complementarian Perspective," in Gundry and Beck, 158.

30. Westfall, *Paul and Gender*, 5.

31. Ibid., 212.

32. This is similar to a concept from constitutional law known as "strict scrutiny." Under a strict scrutiny standard, which applies in cases of certain types of government discrimination (e.g., race), the "government must show an extremely important reason for its action *and* it must demonstrate that the goal cannot be achieved through any less discriminatory alternative." Erwin Chemerinsky, *Constitutional Law: Principles and Policies*, 3rd ed. (New York: Aspen, 2006), 694–95.

This is the most stringent constitutional test available, one that requires the government to meet the heavy burden of demonstrating that the discrimination is necessary to "achieve a compelling government purpose." I believe the church would be well served by adopting a "strict scrutiny" standard (or something like it) with respect to imposing gender-based limits on the use of spiritual gifts within the body of Christ.

33. The moral consequences of prohibiting women from widely developing and using their spiritual gifts must be taken into account as a matter of practical theology. Some might object that this is an improper appeal to consequences, an informal logical fallacy known as *argumentum ad consequentiam* that involves accepting a belief to be either true or false based upon whether it leads to desirable consequences. But that is not the case here. In this scenario, multiple passages of Scripture indicate that the consequences of using one's gifts are of the utmost importance. The focus on consequences arises in this instance because egalitarians are making a *reductio ad absurdum* argument in response to conservative complementarians. Specifically, egalitarians are attempting to show that the conservative complementarian interpretation of 1 Timothy 2:9–15 leads to a contradictory result between their "plain reading" of the text and the plain reading of other passages pertaining to the exercise of gifts (e.g., Romans 12 and 1 Peter 4:10–11). As logicians well know, a *reductio* argument isn't fallacious. Egalitarians are making a logical argument based upon hermeneutics, not a fallacious argument based upon personal desires, feelings, or preferences.

34. Thomas R. Schreiner, "An Interpretation of 1 Timothy 2:9–15: A Dialogue with Scholarship," in *Women in the*

Church: An Analysis of 1 Timothy 2:9–15, eds. Andreas J. Köstenberger and Thomas R. Schreiner, 2nd ed. (Grand Rapids, MI: Baker, 2005), 225n210.

35. Westfall, *Paul and Gender*, 219.
36. We see early hints of a growing Pauline corpus—a collection of Paul's letters—in Colossians 4:16 and 2 Peter 3:15–16.
37. Klein, Blomberg, and Hubbard, *Introduction to Biblical Interpretation*, 317.
38. Ilan Fuchs, *Jewish Women's Torah Study: Orthodox Religious Education and Modernity* (New York: Routledge, 2014), 167.
39. Westfall articulates this concern: "When experience, emotions, and personal responsibility are removed from the equation, [a woman] must go to an authority or mediator to perceive her call for her, to hear God's voice, and to figure out what her function is. Each woman is incapacitated in determining her gift according to the grace given her. The 'plain' sense of Romans 12:1–8 is canceled. In practice, a man's experience and emotions are treated as normative in his call to ministry, but a woman's emotions and experience are treated as suspect and can be invalidated if they lead her to a place that is outside of wherever the male authorities draw the line delimiting the appropriate sphere of ministry for women.... But... there are two primary determinants of gifts and function: the realistic estimation of the individual, and the Holy Spirit, who gives gifts to every individual just as he determines (1 Cor. 12:11). This argues against the theology of 'drawing a line' and creating a priori rules of how God works that cancel out the clear theology of the passages on gifting in regard to women." Westfall, *Paul and Gender*, 215.

40. Stanley J. Grenz, "Biblical Priesthood and Women in Ministry," in Pierce and Groothuis, 283.

41. Complementarian Douglas Moo believes that the activity of teaching is inherently authoritative if it is regarding the Word of God, thus women should never teach the Bible to adult men. Consequently, if you're a woman who wants to teach adult men about taxidermy in a Sunday school class, then go for it. Douglas Moo, "What Does It Mean Not to Teach or Have Authority Over Men? 1 Timothy 2:11–15," in Piper and Grudem, 186.

42. Michelle Lee-Barnewall, *Neither Complementarian nor Egalitarian: A Kingdom Corrective to the Evangelical Gender Debate* (Grand Rapids, MI: Baker, 2016), 168–69.

43. Os Guinness, *The Call: Finding and Fulfilling the Central Purpose of Your Life* (Nashville, TN: Thomas Nelson, 2003), 46.

44. The presence of false teachers is suggested by 1 Timothy 1:3–11; 4:1–5; 6:3–5.

45. *Henry V*, act 4, scene 8.

Chapter 9

1. C. S. Lewis, *The Weight of Glory* (San Francisco: HarperSanFrancisco, 1980), 26.

2. C. S. Lewis, "Mere Christianity," in *The Complete C. S. Lewis Signature Classics* (New York: HarperCollins, 2002), 95.

3. William Temple, *Readings in St. John's Gospel* (London: Macmillan, 1940), 68, as quoted in Ravi Zacharias, "The Church's Role in Apologetics and the Development of the Mind," in *Beyond Opinion*, ed. Ravi Zacharias (Nashville: Thomas Nelson, 2007), 326.

4. However, due to my love for nineties' music, I *will* make time for the rock group The Wallflowers, especially Jakob Dylan's song "One Headlight."
5. Timothy Keller, "Studies in 2 Peter: The Dangerous God (2 Peter 3:1–13)" (MP3 podcast), August 22, 1993, accessed January 29, 2018, https://gospelinlife.com/downloads/studies-in-2-peter/.
6. Timothy Keller, "Spiritual Gifts and Graces" (MP3 podcast), February 7, 2000, accessed May 15, 2018, https://gospelinlife.com/downloads/spiritual-gifts-and-graces-4601/.
7. Clay Jones, *Why Does God Allow Evil? Compelling Answers for Life's Toughest Questions* (Eugene, OR: Harvest House, 2017), 189–206.
8. I'm only able to write now because I was raised in a loving, two-parent home; was educated to the college level; married a spouse who earns enough income that I don't have to work full-time outside the home; and many other factors known and unknown to me. I owe much to those who have supported me and helped me to care for my children.
9. Rebecca Manley Pippert, *Out of the Salt Shaker and into the World: Evangelism as a Way of Life*, 2nd ed. (Downers Grove, IL: InterVarsity, 1999), 245.
10. Lewis, *The Weight of Glory*, 45.
11. "Making us dignified, despite the indignities we visit on one another, is an ongoing spiritual process. That's why the Bible describes each of us as God's 'workmanship, created in Christ Jesus for good works' (Ephesians 2:10). The two words, *workmanship* and *created,* are not interchangeable. *Workmanship* is translated from the Greek word *poiema*, which means anything brought into existence or compiled

by someone. It's where we get the English word *poem* from. You and I—all of us—are God's poem." Abdu Murray, *Saving Truth: Finding Meaning and Clarity in a Post-Truth World* (Grand Rapids, MI: Zondervan, 2018), 115.

Acknowledgements

Thank you to all of the scholars who devoted time and energy into researching this topic, and in particular to those whom I have referenced in this book. This project would not have been completed without the feedback from some of my close friends and first readers: Christy Patterson-Hamilton, Lauren Frederick, Christina Painter, and Nathan Hamilton. Their encouragement gave me the fortitude to press on in spite of the unconventional nature of the project. This book would be far less organized without the keen editorial skills of the very gifted Lori Vanden Bosch. I'm indebted to Amanda Halash for sharing her wisdom about the publishing industry with me, and to Denny and Sara Williams for their many years of friendship throughout my life. I'm grateful to Frank Mitchell for his keen insights regarding principles-based approaches to designing efficient processes.

More than any other person, my husband Randy has encouraged, supported, inspired, and as needed, challenged me through this project from beginning to end. Once he caught the vision for encouraging the use of spiritual gifts in the body of Christ, he never wavered in his sacrificial love through it all. To my two kind sons, please know that I love you very much. I hope that I didn't miss too much "precious playing time" away from you while completing this project. Finally, and most importantly, I want to thank our loving and gracious God for all that I am and all that I have. I sincerely pray that this effort will bring Him glory and edify my brothers and sisters in Christ.

Further Reading

Clouse, Bonnidell and Robert G. Clouse, eds. *Women in Ministry: Four Views*. Downers Grove, IL: InterVarsity, 1989.

Groothuis, Rebecca M. *Good News for Women: A Biblical Picture of Gender Equality*. Grand Rapids, MI: Baker, 1997.

Guinness, Os. *The Call: Finding and Fulfilling the Central Purpose of Your Life*. Nashville: Thomas Nelson, 2003.

Gundry, Stanley N. and James R. Beck, eds. *Two Views on Women in Ministry*. Rev. ed. Grand Rapids, MI: Zondervan, 2005.

Huffman, Douglas S., ed. *How Then Should We Choose? Three Views on God's Will and Decision Making*. Grand Rapids, MI: Kregel, 2009.

Keener, Craig S. *Paul, Women and Wives: Marriage and Women's Ministry in the Letters of Paul*. Peabody, MA: Hendrickson, 1992.

Klein, William W., Craig L. Blomberg, and Robert L. Hubbard, Jr. *Introduction to Biblical Interpretation*. 3rd ed. Grand Rapids, MI: Zondervan, 2017.

Köstenberger, Andreas J. and Thomas R. Schreiner, eds. *Women in the Church: An Interpretation and Application of 1 Timothy 2:9–15*. 3rd ed. Wheaton, IL: Crossway, 2016.

Lee-Barnewall, Michelle. *Neither Complementarian nor Egalitarian: A Kingdom Corrective to the Evangelical Gender Debate*. Grand Rapids, MI: Baker, 2016.

Nielson, Kathleen. *Women and God: Hard Questions, Beautiful Truth*. Denmark: The Good Book Company, 2018.

Pierce, Ronald W. and Rebecca M. Groothuis, eds. *Discovering Biblical Equality: Complementarity without Hierarchy*. Downers Grove, IL: InterVarsity, 2005.

Piper, John and Wayne Grudem, eds. *Recovering Biblical Manhood and Womanhood: A Response to Evangelical Feminism*. Wheaton, IL: Crossway, 2006.

Saucy, Robert L. and Judith K. TenElshof, eds. *Women and Men in Ministry: A Complementary Perspective*. Chicago: Moody, 2001.

Sumner, Sarah. *Men and Women in the Church: Building Consensus on Christian Leadership*. Downers Grove, IL: InterVarsity, 2003.

Westfall, Cynthia L. *Paul and Gender: Reclaiming the Apostle's Vision for Men and Women in Christ*. Grand Rapids, MI: Baker, 2016.

Made in the USA
Lexington, KY
30 August 2018